D0832774

Living with a
Golden
Retriever

Edited by Sally Stewart

RINGPRESS

Photo courtesy: The Frisbie kennels, USA.

The Question of Gender
The 'he' pronoun is used throughout this book in favour of the rather
impersonal 'it', but no gender bias is intended at all.

Published by Ringpress Books Ltd,
PO Box 8, Lydney,
Gloucestershire GL15 4YN

Series Director: Claire Horton-Bussey

Designed by Rob Benson.

First Published 2000
© 2000 RINGPRESS BOOKS

ISBN 1 86054 103 8

Printed and bound in Singapore through Printworks International Limited

0 9 8 7 6 5 4 3 2 1

CONTENTS

CHAPTER ONE

INTRODUCING THE GOLDEN RETRIEVER

They say blondes have more fun, and, as far as the Golden Retriever is concerned, this is certainly true. The Golden has a smile to melt most hearts and a cheery temperament to match. This is not to say that life with a Golden is always easy. Someone once said that a Golden Retriever enters the world as a puppy and leaves it as a puppy, too. Most mature eventually, but it does not take much to unleash their effervescence – so be warned!

Amiable, friendly, and easy-going, it's no wonder the Golden Retriever is a popular choice; in both the UK and North America it ranks among the top five of all pedigree breeds. Loyal and entertaining, there can be no better companion or family dog.

Aristocratic Origins

The Golden Retriever is quite a newcomer to the canine world, at least compared to some breeds which can be traced back thousands of years. Goldens never sat at the feet of Pharaohs, as the Pharaoh Hound did, nor do they feature in ancient Persian and Roman literature, as the Mastiff does, but the breed's roots are every bit as distinguished – the founding father of the breed was a British lord.

It was originally believed that the breed was discovered by the first Lord Tweedmouth, Dudley Coutts Marjoribanks (pronounced 'Marshbanks'), who was so enchanted with some performing Russian circus dogs, he bought them all and took them up to Guisachan, his extensive Scottish country estate.

Sadly, this romantic tale has been discredited, following the discovery that the breed is of Scottish, not Russian, origin. It is now believed that Lord Tweedmouth bought a yellow retriever from a cobbler after seeing the dog walking through the streets of Brighton, in the south of England. The cobbler had been given the dog as payment for a debt owed to him by an employee of Lord Chichester's estate. The dog, which Lord Tweedmouth named 'Nous' (Gaelic for 'wisdom'), is said to have been the only yellow dog from a litter of black, wavy-coated puppies born in 1864.

Lord Tweedmouth was a keen sportsman, and shooting parties were a great feature of life at Guisachan. Nous proved his worth retrieving birds, and so he became the forefather of a new breed specifically developed as a working gundog. From Lord Tweedmouth's stud book, which is now held by the Kennel Club in London, we can see that Nous was mated to a Tweed Water Spaniel – a now extinct breed which has been likened to an American Water Spaniel with retriever features (taller, less feathering, shorter ears). The first mating took place in 1868 to a bitch called Belle, who went on to produce four puppies: a dog called Crocus, and two bitches called Cowslip and Primrose. A third bitch called Ada was believed to have been the fourth pup, but evidence suggests she was actually from Nous and Belle's second litter, in 1872. The Tweedmouth gundogs were greatly admired, and many were given as gifts to use on other large shooting estates. Ada, for example, was given to Lord Tweedmouth's nephew, the fifth Earl of Ilchester, who established his own pedigree line.

The Golden Retriever was developed to be the ultimate shooting companion, retrieving over land and water.

Setter blood was used to develop the breed, as well as various wavy-coated retrievers. Although black dogs were used in the initial breeding programmes, yellow offspring were often produced. It was noted that mating a black dog and a yellow bitch produced yellow pups, though a yellow dog and a black bitch produced both colours.

A big breakthrough for the breed came in the 1880s when the first dogs were taken to America by the youngest son of Lord Tweedmouth. He took Belle and Nous' descendants – Lady and Sol – with him when he moved to Texas to run the family ranch.

The Retriever's Role

Why was the new breed so successful as a working gundog? The reason is quite simple – it was all about being in the right place at the right time.

In the days when nets and hawks were used to trap birds, the hunter had no need of a retriever. Since the 1500s, flushing spaniels have been employed to agitate game from cover so the falconer's hawk could be sent in for the kill. Setting spaniels (which were later developed into setters) were used to find the game and creep up on it, to indicate to the hunter where he should throw his net.

When muzzle-loading guns were first used, it was very much a hit and miss affair, and hunters were more than capable of collecting the half a dozen or so close-range birds targeted. Some spaniels, setters and pointers were used to retrieve game, but it was the introduction and development of the single-trigger breech-loading gun during the latter half of the 19th century, that overturned the whole shooting tradition.

For the first time, hunters were able to shoot birds on the wing, and even more importantly, they were able to shoot vast numbers of them. With more birds being killed over a wider radius, hunters could not keep a track of where the birds had fallen, and it became too time-consuming to go in search of them. A keen retriever, who would work over land and water was urgently required – and Lord Tweedmouth's dogs were developed to fit the bill.

At the same time the railway network expanded, making travel easier. The aristocracy would visit each other's country estates for shooting parties, and reliable gundogs were needed to fetch the fallen fowl. The time was ripe for the Golden Retriever's dramatic rise in popularity.

Water Babies

The Golden Retriever was bred to have the temperament, the ability, and the 'looks' that would serve his purpose as a hunting companion. Built on athletic lines, the Golden was developed to have the power and stamina to work all day in the field. His glorious coat was not simply bred for cosmetic reasons – a hardy

Goldens have a natural affinity with water.

gundog needed an equally hardy coat to protect against the cold and wet when out working, and to prevent injury to the dog when running through briar and gorse, searching for game. Although the shade of 'gold' varies considerably, most working strains are dark in colour which acts as better camouflage.

When the first Lord Tweedmouth bred the yellow retriever with a Tweed Water Spaniel, he not only created a new breed with a waterproof coat, he also introduced the qualities of a good water dog, to ensure the Golden Retriever would be as keen to dive into a cold, muddy lake to retrieve a bird, as he would be to dive

The 'waterproof' coat is a breed characteristic.

into the undergrowth. Golden owners will bear witness to the fact that modern-day examples continue the legacy and are only too keen to leap into water – however dirty – at any opportunity!

Working Heritage

Breeders today still aim to preserve the Golden's original features, which were his 'tools for his job'. For example, without strong jaws and a perfect, regular and complete scissor bite, the Golden would not be able to retrieve fallen game with a 'soft mouth'. This was a crucial function in a retriever. It was all well and good to have the perfect dog who would search out

and fetch game, but if an over-eager Golden with imperfect dentition then rendered it inedible, all efforts would have been wasted. Everyone who has ever owned a Golden will talk of the breed's great propensity for carrying things in its mouth – toys, car keys, bowls, bottles, wallets – it may not be fallen game, but the Golden still believes he has a duty to carry it!

Kind, confident and trustworthy, the Golden's people-friendly characteristics ensured he had the right disposition to be trained to retrieve, and to work closely with the hunter, and this close interaction with his human owners is one of the Golden's greatest assets.

The Breed Today

The Golden Retriever is still widely used as a working gundog, and is highly-prized for the zest and enthusiasm he brings to his work.

Biddable and intelligent, the Golden has also proved himself in other spheres. The breed is widely used as a guide dog for the blind, a dog for the disabled, and as a hearing dog for the deaf.

For those owners who enjoy training, the Golden is a talented competitor in Working Trials, Competitive Obedience and Agility and Flyball, and for those who relish the glamour of the show ring, the gorgeous Golden will always prove a head-turner.

Today, with the vast majority of Goldens living in pet homes, the breed's friendly, bright temperament has secured its position as one of the most popular breeds of dogs in many parts of the world.

The Golden takes great delight in carrying things in its mouth.

CHAPTER TWO

PUPPY POWER

After months of careful research into which breed you should choose, travelling miles to find the ideal breeder, ensuring your house and garden are fully puppy-proofed, deciding on a dog or a bitch, and, lastly, picking the individual puppy from a litter, you finally have the little fella home. Now the hard work – and the fun – really starts...

FAMILY LIFE

Loyal, fun-loving and affectionate, the Golden Retriever is renowned for being a great family dog. He loves being surrounded by people and taking part in family activities.

A puppy at heart, the Golden has a tremendous sense of fun and enjoys playing with children.

However, as with all dogs and children, care must be taken. A puppy that has been brought up with his littermates has learnt to play rough, and his manners need to be refined so that he

does not, unintentionally, hurt small children by jumping up and mouthing. Equally, children tend to get over-excited – and waving arms may be misinterpreted. For this reason, small children and dogs should always be supervised by a responsible adult. This gives the opportunity to teach both puppy and child a sense of mutual respect. It is your task to work on the following 'Golden' rules:

- A puppy is not a toy to be played with incessantly.
- A puppy needs to be allowed to rest undisturbed. A tired puppy is an irritable puppy, and unacceptable behaviour such as growling or even biting may result.
- House rules – not begging for food, not lying on the sofa, etc. – must be enforced by all the family, or the puppy will get inconsistent messages.
- A puppy must be taught how to play with children – e.g. jumping up and mouthing is not permitted.

It will help if the breeder has already started the process of socialising the puppies. A puppy that has been raised with children, or has had some contact with them, will be more ready to fit into family life.

If you do not have any children of your own, it is still important that your Golden gets used to them. Perhaps you have grandchildren who visit occasionally, or maybe you baby-sit for neighbours. Even if your life is completely child-free, you are always going to encounter them when you take your dog out, so it's best to be prepared.

Ask friends to bring children on visits, and ensure the pup has a really good time playing with them. Goldens are not nervous dogs if they are introduced to new experiences carefully, and from a young age. Since they have an innate love of people, there should be few problems integrating your Golden into family life.

Child's Play

The pup has to learn that he is the bottom of the pack and that small people have to be obeyed too. To help reinforce this, ensure all members of the family, even the youngest ones, have basic control over the pup. Make sure that children are included in training sessions and can master basic obedience with your new Golden. It is important that all members of the family use the same words for commands, otherwise the puppy can easily get confused.

Exercise One

The food bowl can be a particular area of contention between children and dogs. If your dog does not consider himself to be the least important creature in the house, he may guard his bowl if children are around, fearing they are competing for his grub. This can be prevented from an early stage:

Your puppy must learn not to be possessive about his food.

Teach your puppy to take treats "gently".

- Allow a child to feed the pup by putting small amounts of food into his bowl.
- Far from dreading a small hand reaching out for the bowl, the pup will soon welcome it, associating it with food being added, not taken away.

Exercise Two

It is natural for puppies to mouth when young. However, you must ensure your pup develops good bite-inhibition so that he grows up knowing that teeth must never make contact with flesh.

- If your puppy does mouth a child – or anyone else for that matter – when playing, instruct the child to respond with a loud, sharp yelp.
- The pup should then be ignored.
- Your Golden will soon learn that mouthing people, especially children, causes pain and results in being temporarily ostracised from the pack.

This action mirrors the bitch's reaction to being bitten when playing with her pups.

Exercise Three

If your Golden has contact with children, he must learn the "Gently" command. He must take treats gently, play gently, and must not jump up. Not only does this instil good manners in your Golden but it prevents accidents later on – a puppy grows much more quickly than a child and will not realise his own strength when fully grown.

- Start with a treat in your hand and offer it to the dog, asking him to take it "Gently".
- If he snaps, or attempts to take it roughly, yelp sharply as if in pain, and do not give it to him – just keep hold of it.
- Do not take it away altogether or your pup will be even more eager to take it quickly when it reappears.
- Repeat the command "Gently", only giving the treat when he takes it from your hand with extreme care.
- Repeat the exercise regularly until it is second nature to him. You can then move on to training the pup to take treats gently from children.

Exercise Four

Another exercise to practise with children is to make your Golden comfortable with hands reaching over his head to grab his collar. Some dogs can find this action quite intimidating and may snap if threatened. Get your pup accustomed to this action while he is still very young and, again, make it an enjoyable experience.

- Sit with your puppy, giving treats, while using your free hand to feel his collar every now and again.
- The pup's attention will probably be so fixed on the hand with the treats, he is unlikely to be bothered by what the other hand is doing.
- As before, when your Golden is perfectly happy with you doing this, get a child to repeat the exercise, stressing that treats should be taken "Gently".

Training Children

When raising a pup, it may also be a case of training your children, too – which can be a more difficult task! Children must be taught to respect the pup's need for his own space and to be careful they do not endlessly over-excite him.

If you have badly behaved children, you may find breeders are unwilling to sell you a pup. This is not necessarily from fear of the pup being harmed by children being too rough, but because it reflects badly on your training skills: if your kids are naughty through lack of discipline, the pup is likely to turn out the same way.

If there are any problems at all between your dog and children, take no chances and consult an animal behaviourist immediately. Your vet should be able to recommend someone suitable.

THE 'EXTENDED' FAMILY

Similar care and attention should also be

Both child and puppy must learn to respect each other.

exercised when introducing your Golden to other household residents, such as other dogs or cats. Although the Golden is a gundog, with strong hunting and retrieving instincts, he is also supremely loyal – and that includes loyalty to all members of the household, even non-human ones. Of course, care must be taken with introductions, but he usually takes to his own clan quite quickly – whether it includes cats, rabbits, chickens or goats.

As with all relationships, longterm trouble is usually avoided if things get off on the right footing. A boisterous puppy may intend no harm, but he could appear very frightening to a smaller animal such as a cat. Plan a controlled introduction using the following guidelines.

- The puppy should be restrained, either by holding him, or by attaching a collar and lead (if the puppy's training has reached this stage). Ask another family member to cuddle the cat while you bring the dog into the room.
- The cat must be reassured as the puppy approaches, and discouraged from trying to run away. Keep your Golden as calm as possible and let both cat and puppy have a good sniff at each other.
- When the dog calms down and stops trying to leap on his feline friend, praise him and give a treat. You should also reward your Golden when he actually ignores the cat.

'Your Golden will quickly adapt to his family circle'

Some people use indoor crates to confine the cat for short introductory periods. Moving the cat and crate around different rooms also ensures that the cat's smell is distributed around the house and therefore becomes more familiar to the dog. However, this measure is not generally necessary with a Golden. Once he understands that the cat is part of his family, he is usually okay – and the odd swipe around the nose from the cat's paw if he does overstep the mark, soon teaches him some manners.

Obviously there are always exceptions (especially with dogs from strong working strains), so monitor how your Golden reacts before you are confident enough to leave him unsupervised with other pets. If you have other animals, use the same process of supervised introductions, and your Golden will quickly adapt to his new family circle.

OUTSIDE THE HOME

With animals that do not 'belong' to the family, such as rabbits encountered on a walk, your Golden is likely to show more interest, as most dogs will, and may well chase. More often than not, however, he will come back with nothing – the spirit is willing, but the flesh just is not fast enough! It is important to ensure that you have good control over your dog, so you can command a recall if he starts disappearing into the distance in hot pursuit. (See Recall, page 29).

With other dogs that he may encounter on his walks, a well-socialised Golden Retriever will very rarely start a fight, nor hang about to finish one. There are always exceptions, but as a breed, the Golden is friendly with other dogs and eager to play with them.

However, it can be intimidating for a nervous dog to be met with an over-enthusiastic Golden trying to start a game and this could result in your well-intentioned pet being growled at, or worse. Goldens do not usually have any hang-ups or dominance problems, so the majority will accept the telling-off and leave well alone.

With good obedience control over your dog, you will be able to call him to you the moment you see him approaching a dog that is not interested in socialising. Make sure you do not restrict his social activities altogether, though. If he realises he will get called back whenever he approaches another dog, he may become reluctant to respond to your commands, knowing that his obedience will simply be rewarded by being put on the lead. Most dogs love playing with others, and those that should be avoided are definitely in the minority.

TWO'S COMPANY
If you are considering taking on another

With a little tact and diplomacy, the established dog will soon learn to accept the new arrival.

Golden, you must select the pup with as much care as your initial dog – finding a good, responsible breeder who does all the relevant tests (see Chapter Eight), who rears in the home, and who gives after-sales advice and support for the puppy's entire life.

With Golden Retrievers you would be well-advised to choose the opposite sex to your existing dog. Although Goldens usually live quite contentedly with dogs of the same sex (unlike some other breeds), there can be problems, so it is wise to avoid same-sex combinations.

With two males, dominance problems may emerge when the puppy becomes a troublesome teenager keen to exert his new-found authority and to challenge the existing top-dog (see Chapter Three).

Two bitches can be even more troublesome – particularly when hormones play havoc with behaviour during the seasonal cycle. Problem relationships between bitches may occur only in a minority of cases, but they usually end in heart-break. It is estimated that in 70 per cent of problem cases, one of the bitches has to be rehomed.

Obviously, if you have a male and a female dog, you will need to consider neutering one or both of them to prevent unwanted puppies.

Generation Gap

In the vast majority of cases, your established dog will learn to love your new Golden just as much as you do. But don't leave it to chance. To avoid the new dog stepping on territorial toes,

' It is only natural to feel sorry for the under-dog. '

arrange for the introduction to take place on neutral ground – a park, for example (remember that he must be vaccinated before being taken to public places). Your back garden is not ideal, as your existing dog will consider it to be as much his property as your house.

Allow the dogs to play, but do not introduce any toys just yet as your existing dog may feel the need to defend them from the new dog. After establishing who is top-dog, and having sniffed, played, and sniffed some more, your Goldens should have laid the foundations of a secure future friendship – without anyone feeling threatened. When you finally return home, your existing dog will be inviting his new friend in, too, rather than having a pup foisted upon him without as much as a courteous how-d'you-do.

A boisterous, energetic pup, who is fussed and adored by all members of the family, can be quite disconcerting to an older, established dog, who was formerly the centre of attention. To avoid jealousy, make as much fuss of your existing dog as of your new acquisition, and always reinforce his position. If he growls at the over-excitable Golden pup for chewing his tail once too often, do not interfere; if you do, you will be undermining his superior ranking.

It is only natural to feel sorry for the under-dog, especially if it is a defenceless-looking little pup; but fussing and favouring him over the top-dog is confusing to both, as you will be elevating the under-dog's position. Remember: dogs are social animals and are used to hierarchies. If you have a top-dog and an under-dog, and they are both happy with their position, that is great. Do not anthropomorphise – liberating the under-dog from the 'shackles of domination' – as this will only throw the carefully balanced power structure into chaos.

Make sure you reinforce the dogs' chosen rankings at every opportunity. Feed and praise the top-dog first, let him through doors before the under-dog, and so on. These may not seem important actions to us, but in canine language, it indicates in no uncertain terms who is boss.

Many people get a puppy when they have a veteran dog, believing the pup can be taught some good manners by the old-timer. Yes, in some cases, established dogs do tutor the youngster, but in other cases, the pup can lead the older dog astray. Then you have double the trouble. Others get a pup hoping it will give the Golden oldie a new lease of life. However, older dogs can be less tolerant, and are certainly much less active than irrepressible Golden puppies whose batteries never seem to run out. An indoor crate can be useful as a den for your pup or older dog to retreat to if they need time away

Vigilance is the key to house-training.

from the other (see Crate-training).

HOUSE-TRAINING

Pups are pre-programmed to be clean: they will always defecate and urinate away from their sleeping and eating areas. House-training is just a case of encouraging them to perform where you would like them to. Goldens are bright dogs, and it won't take long for your pup to realise that you would much prefer him to defecate in a designated spot in the garden. Use a verbal command, such as "Be clean", when your pup obliges, and he will soon associate the words with the appropriate action.

The moment your Golden eliminates on your chosen spot outside, praise him so he is left in no uncertain terms that he has done something worthy of celebration. It may be difficult to whip up enthusiasm about such a basic body function – but consider the alternative: a pup that treats your house like a lavatory for months on end.

Praise, treat and play each time your pup performs outside. Never return to the house immediately afterwards or he may be reluctant to eliminate, knowing that his time outside soon comes to an end afterwards.

Avoiding 'Accidents'

If your pup has an accident, the only creature you should shout at is yourself. The pup is not to blame; it is your fault for not being sufficiently vigilant. A young pup must be taken outside to the garden frequently, especially after waking, playing, exercising and feeding. As soon as you see him sniffing the ground, often pacing in circling movements, you can bet he is trying to find a suitable spot to eliminate, so whisk him outside.

If you catch him in mid-flow, some trainers recommend startling the pup so he stops, giving you time to get him outside. Training disks, pebbles in a can, or car keys can be used to make a sudden noise. Avoid shouting to startle him, or scaring him with the noise you make, as you do not want the pup to fear going to the toilet in front of you. If this happens, he may become reluctant even to eliminate outside when you are present. This will lead to the pup trying to go to the toilet secretly when you are not around.

Once the pup's vaccinations are complete, take the time to train him in other places, on different surfaces.

Some dogs will only ever perform in their garden, which can cause them a lot of distress if they are taken out for the day. Get him used to sand, grass, gravel, concrete and any other kind of ground he may need to use.

Make sure you always take poop-scoop bags with you so you are equipped to clear up after your dog wherever you are. Dog mess is never pleasant: bag it and bin it, so others do not have to encounter it.

CRATE-TRAINING

Indoor crates are now widely used, and many dog owners find them an invaluable training aid. The idea is to make the crate a 'doggie den' where your puppy feels safe and secure, and can rest undisturbed. It is also useful during house-training. A puppy is reluctant to soil his own bed, and will quickly learn to wait until he is released and taken out to the garden.

The crate should be used to restrict the puppy for short periods – if you have workmen in, or anti-dog friends are visiting – but never let your Golden view his crate as a prison where he spends hours in solitary confinement.

Generally, Goldens do not seem as keen on crates as most other breeds. They are such sociable animals that they are not so inclined to take themselves off for a bit of peace and quiet. The loving Golden prefers to stay close by his family. For this reason, it is a good idea to locate

An indoor crate will prove to be a wise investment.

the crate in the living room or the kitchen, where there is likely to be company.

Putting your Golden in a crate occasionally, and getting him accustomed to being away from you, is also useful for avoiding separation anxiety in the future. Although your pup would like to spend every minute of every day with you, he must learn to be confident when alone. (See Chapter Three.)

If you plan to use a crate when your Golden is fully grown, make sure you buy one that is big enough. A good comfortable size would be 42in (length) x 26in (width) x 30in height (106.5cm x 66cm x 76cm). Crates should contain comfortable washable bedding, and some of your dog's favourite toys, so he can chew, play or sleep as he pleases. Some crates come with an attached puppy pen, so your Golden has space to move around while still being secure.

CAR TRAVEL

Being portable, crates can also be used to take your Golden out safely in the car. Never let your pup travel unrestrained: it is dangerous for him and for the driver. Every year, dogs are killed in car accidents when they are propelled from the rear of cars through the windscreen. Sometimes the impact is so great that they can kill the driver or front passenger. Those dogs that do survive can run off, terrified, never to be found again.

If you do not use a crate in the car, buy a special car harness (available from most pet stores) which safely secures your pet to the back seat.

'A car ride is a joy to most Goldens'

Joy Ride

It is important that your pup realises that all roads do not lead to the vet surgery. He needs to be shown that cars are fun:

- Place the crate in the back of the car and pop the pup in it, with the door open. Stay with him, give him a treat and perhaps encourage him to play with one of his toys.
- Over the course of a few sessions, increase the length of time that the pup is in the crate. Progress to shutting the crate and starting the engine, and give lots of praise and reassurance. The puppy will soon realise that the car is a great place to be – where there are treats and toys and fuss. And, of course, it usually ends in an exciting walk.
- Start with very short journeys and gradually extend the length of time that he is in the car. It is especially important to get your pup used to car travel if you are thinking of showing him in the future.

Goldens usually love car journeys. It is quite usual for pups to get car-sick in the early days, but most grow out of it fairly quickly. If your Golden is prone to car-sickness, make sure he has not eaten immediately before a journey. Car-sickness remedies are available from your vet. There are homoeopathic alternatives, too. For example, many people have had success with ginger, giving one ginger biscuit prior to the journey. Some breeders recommend taking the pup for short journeys in the middle of the night, which is said, inexplicably, to work.

Hot Dogs

When travelling with your dog, always remain aware of temperature changes. If it is a long journey, your dog should always have access to fresh water (non-spillable bowls are invaluable), and you should open a window to get air into the car, too. Put some material on the top of the crate to prevent the sun beating down through glass straight on to the dog, and make frequent stops if necessary.

Never leave a dog in a car. The inside of a car can quickly become like a furnace, even in overcast weather, and many canine victims die every year. Even if you park in the shade, temperatures can still soar, and the sun will change position during the time that the car is left. Equally, a cloudy day can quickly become a scorcher. Do not take a chance on your dog's life: either leave him safely at home, or take him with you to your destination.

SOCIALISATION

Your Golden will be very inquisitive as a pup, so make the most of this and introduce him to as many new experiences as you can. In the first weeks, before your pup has been fully inoculated, this should include getting used to household appliances, like the television, the vacuum cleaner and the washing machine. This is a process the breeder should have started.

Ask visitors to come wearing hats, crash helmets, sunglasses or headphones. Carry an

Expose your puppy to a variety of experiences while his mind is at its most receptive.

umbrella around in the garden, and act as if there is nothing to be afraid of. If you act nervously, your astute Golden pup will soon pick up your negativity and will believe there *is* something to fear.

Once your puppy has experienced a variety of different situations, he will develop a calm outlook. He will see the world as a safe place, with nothing to fear.

Once your pup has been fully inoculated, enrol your Golden in a course of good puppy socialisation classes. Go along without your dog before deciding which one to attend, and monitor the methods used.

- Are the instructors gentle with the dogs?
- Do they use rewards instead of force?
- Would you feel comfortable taking your pup to this class?

Remember that the pup is not the only one being trained – you also have to be alert, learning how to continue raising your Golden.

Many owners make the mistake of believing that training is finished once the course is completed – in fact, it is ongoing throughout your Golden's life. The classes are crucial for laying the foundations and for introducing your pup to other doggie pals so he learns how to interact; but you must continue building on the early lessons of socialisation and training.

MEAN MACHINES

If the vacuum cleaner has your Golden running for cover, there are measures you can take.

- Put the appliance in the corner of a room and leave it unplugged. Your pup may be very wary of it initially, but distract him with games, and ignore the fact that it is there.
- When your Golden is able to walk past the vacuum confidently (this may take hours or even days), progress to switching it on very briefly.
- Initially, you may need someone to do this while you play with him, fuss him and give him tasty treats. Your puppy may be startled to begin with, but keep him occupied. If he is busy trying to get his favourite liver rewards from your hand, the cleaner should be only a passing distraction.
- Turn the vacuum on and off repeatedly. When he no longer reacts to it being switched on, then you can increase the length of time it is left on.
- When he is fully confident with the sound, then you can repeat the whole process – this time vacuuming a small area at a time until he accepts it being moved around the floor, too.

The worst thing you can do is to avoid vacuuming around your dog – the longer it takes to overcome his fear, the worse it will become. If your Golden keeps encountering his fear and realises there is nothing to be afraid of, the phobia should diminish.

Give plenty of reassurance if your puppy shows signs of nervousness when confronted with something new – like the vacuum cleaner.

One Golden owner, for example, had a pup that was scared of buses, so she took the dog and a deckchair to a busy bus station and sat there all day, reassuring the dog. Several hours later (after many odd looks from the public), she had a calm, confident dog that has never so much as blinked at a bus since.

Provide suitable toys that your puppy is allowed to chew.

You should take your Golden pup on the bus or on a train, and get him used to going down a busy high street – anywhere where he is likely to encounter new experiences.

Monitor your Golden's reactions to each new situation. If introduced at a young enough age, your puppy will accept everything as being quite normal. He is a blank canvas, ready to accept as much information as possible. It is natural that he may display caution at some new experiences. Remain with him, and, again, act confidently as if there is nothing to be afraid of. If he is truly terrified, do not force him to stay. Just try again later or review your plan (see 'Mean Machines', above).

ESCHEWING CHEWING

All puppies chew. Like babies, pups get a lot of enjoyment from investigating things orally – from slippers, sofas and table legs, through to plants, jewellery and the contents of the ashtray. As adults, Goldens are usually very soft-mouthed, but being such a food-oriented breed, Golden pups can be worse chewers than many other breeds, so be prepared for 24-hour vigilance and keep all 'valuables' out of reach.

A pup has no idea of the destruction he is causing, so do not shout and yell – just be more careful next time. A dog is also unaware of potential hazards, so you must puppy-proof your home. Few owners consider that the innocuous-looking spider plant in the bathroom is the cause of their pup's vomiting and that the mistletoe in the garden can cause vomiting and diarrhoea, culminating in death from heart failure in just a couple of hours.

To prevent tragedy, look at your house and garden from a puppy's level. Whatever is reachable, is chewable. Either remove it or bar your dog access to it. If you suspect your Golden has swallowed something poisonous, call your vet immediately and take along a sample of whatever it is your dog may have swallowed to show the vet when your dog is examined.

Remember also that dogs can leap astonishing heights and crawl through the tiniest of spaces, so make sure your garden is secure and surrounded with a six-foot fence. Your puppy should be safely identified, too, in case he does ever manage to escape.

Identity discs, coupled with a permanent form of identification (such as microchips, tattoos), will increase the likelihood of your being reunited with your pet.

Of course, you do not want your Golden to stop chewing altogether. Puppies *should* chew – it helps to relieve the pain of teething and to harden up their gums. Removing all your chewable things and not giving suitable alternatives is cruel. Deprived of appropriate chew-toys, who can blame a teething Golden if he finds his own amusement by peppering your favourite designer suit with holes?

Choosing Chews

There are a wide range of chews and chew-toys available for puppies. Remember that your Golden needs a larger and more sturdy chew-toy than, for example, a Yorkshire Terrier puppy. Make sure you check toys and chews regularly for damage. For example, raw-hide bones that splinter or that become small enough to be swallowed, should be disposed of at once, and replaced with new ones. Likewise, squeaks can

work their way out of a toy and can cause choking.

Goldens love hardy rubber rings and other toys they can retrieve. Never throw a stick or a stone for your dog to fetch. There have been horrific accidents where dogs have ended up with sticks and splinters stuck in their mouths, or have choked on stones that could not be removed in time. The same applies to small balls. Always make sure that toys are too large to be swallowed.

Goldens usually love rope toys, which are good at keeping their teeth clean, but do not be tempted to play tug games with your puppy, at least not until his mouth and teeth have had a chance to grow properly. Even with adults, tug-of-war should be played gently.

' Remember, a growing pup needs lots of fuel '

FEEDING YOUR PUPPY

You must follow the diet sheet provided by breeder. If you wish to change the pup's diet, it must be done gradually. Pups are very sensitive little souls, and the slightest change can result in tummy upsets. Generally, your Golden pup must have measured amounts regularly throughout the day – amounting to about four or five meals each day. Although it may seem as if the whole day is spent feeding your new pet, remember that a growing pup needs a lot of 'fuel' – a five-month-old pup will need more food than an adult Golden.

Gradually increase the amounts (follow manufacturer's guidelines, or your breeder's diet sheet), and reduce the number of feeds. As a

It is vitally important not to over-exercise a growing puppy.

general rule, the number of feeds can be cut to three a day when the pup is about four months old, and then to two a day at about six months of age.

If feeding a complete food (many special puppy varieties are available), you can soften the food with warm water or puppy milk, but make sure you allow it to cool before giving it to the pup.

Soft motions can be a sign of overfeeding, so adjust the amount given accordingly. Of course,

if the pup has diarrhoea or vomiting, or loses interest in his food, you must seek veterinary advice at once.

EXERCISE RESTRAINT

It is very important that you do not over-exercise your Golden pup. Bones need to firm up, so do not let him over-exert himself. Stop your puppy from leaping on and off furniture and restrict access to the stairs, at least until he reaches about six months, when his bones should be stronger. Child stair-gates are invaluable if you do not have a door that can bar access to the stairs.

Build up exercise gradually. With an unvaccinated Golden, playing in the garden is usually sufficient. When he is safe to take out, a 10-minute session on the lead each day should be enough.

Monitor and respond to your pup's needs. If he does 'wall of death' around the living room, he probably needs his exercise extended. Remember: do not overdo it; make sure the longer walks are introduced gradually. Three short walks are better than one long gruelling session where the dog is frog-marched at break-neck speed.

Goldens need to be allowed free-running exercise, especially when they are older. While he is a pup, access to the garden should be sufficient for off-lead exercise. This, and a good game of retrieve – which they will happily do all day if they can – should use up much of your Golden's excess energy and help to tire him out. Do not let your pup off the lead in a public

WORKS A TREAT

Food rewards are great at encouraging your stomach-obsessed Golden to train with you. However, there is nothing worse than seeing an overweight, panting Golden who just cannot enjoy life to the full because he is so... well, full. To avoid killing your Golden with kindness, make sure treats are taken out of his daily food allocation. Use small pieces, which can be eaten quickly, to give your dog a taste and make him want more.

Experiment with different treats to find your dog's favourite. Liver will have some dogs literally leaping through hoops, whereas others would sell their own dam for a chunk of cheese.

When you start getting success with a particular training exercise, it is worth withholding the treat until your Golden does it absolutely perfectly. That way, he will have to keep improving – trying hard to achieve a quicker recall, or a longer wait.

And remember: the way to a dog's heart isn't just via the stomach. Goldens love toys and respond to verbal praise, too; so consider using these equally rewarding methods as alternatives.

---

place, however, until you are confident he will come back when called. (See Recall, page 29.)

Once fully vaccinated, ensure your pup has a good combination of walking on soft and hard ground to keep his nails short. Do not be impatient to take your Golden out on long country walks; there is plenty of time for that when the dog is a little older, and he is physically prepared for such exertions.

EARLY LESSONS

When you bring your Golden puppy home, you need to set your house rules – and stick to them. You need to establish right from the start whether you will allow your Golden on your sofa or bed, or whether you will permit him to beg for food. Be consistent. You cannot allow him on the sofa one day because you fancy a cosy cuddle, and then scold him the next because the vicar is coming for tea and you do not want hairs all over the furniture. Likewise, you only have to give one tiny crumb from your plate, and your dog will be begging by the dining table for the rest of his life – just in case you give in again.

Your Golden is an intelligent dog. He will soon learn rules. If you never give him a bit of your dinner, he will realise that it is a waste of energy even asking you for it. He will learn to lie quietly, waiting for you to finish. If you give a treat after all the plates have been cleared away, to reward him for not begging, this should shape his behaviour, too.

Teaching your dog that "No" means "No" is very useful for making sure you all live in harmony. It is more the tone of your voice that will convey to your dog that he should not continue digging, begging, barking and so on. A deep, stern "No" does not usually have to be repeated, and should stop the dog in his tracks.

Grooming Acceptance

The sooner you teach the dog what is expected of him in terms of handling and grooming, the fewer problems you should encounter as he gets older. For example, a Golden puppy coat does not need very much attention at all, but if he gets used to a grooming routine from an early age, he will learn to accept it without resentment. Every day, give him a quick brush through. Use a comb to work through any tangles, and then brush through the coat with a good-quality rounded bristle brush. Make sure he gets accustomed to the hairdryer too.

Similarly, trying to trim the nails of an adult who is wriggling and trying to escape because he does not like having his feet touched, can be a real nuisance.

A few minutes every week acclimatising a puppy to having his ears, eyes, teeth and nails examined is a worthwhile future investment.

If the nails are too long, trim with guillotine-type nail-clippers.

Be careful to trim just the tip of the nail, or you may cut into the quick of the nail, which will result in bleeding.

If you sound exciting and enthusiastic, your puppy will want to come to you.

TRAINING EXERCISES
Recall

The very first thing your dog needs to learn is that when you call his name, you want his attention at once. Once you have your pup's attention, you can then give your command, such as "Rover, come!". Start your recall training in the garden and do not progress to public areas until he has had all his vaccinations and you are confident that he will not run off as soon as he is off the lead.

When you ask your dog to come to you, it must be in the most exciting and energetic way possible. You have to make sure your Golden really wants to come to you, above all other interesting smells, other dogs, squirrels, or chipmunks. Squat down, with your arms outstretched, waiting for him to leap into them for a hug. Every time he comes when called, fuss and praise him really enthusiastically, giving a small treat.

Gradually walk further away from your dog, until he will come reliably at any distance. Practise getting him to come to you throughout the day – when he is in the kitchen and you want him in the sitting room, for example. Each time, make him feel truly clever and special for coming when asked.

Goldens love people, so you do not usually have to ask twice if you want him to come to you – especially when a tasty treat is involved. The problems begin when you extend your training to the park. Your Golden might love you to bits, but he also has a soft spot for other dogs, children who have ice-creams, joggers, and cyclists. Goldens are such sociable creatures, they just want to say "hello" to everyone.

Your "Rover, come!" command needs to be more exciting than all these other factors. And when he does leave another dog to be with you, he must be suitably rewarded, so he knows it is worth his while next time.

If you cannot fully trust him to come, and fear he will run off into the horizon never to be

> **'Do not make the mistake of repeating commands'**

seen again, you can start your recall exercises on a long line. This is longer than a lead, and will give your dog freedom while you still have control of him. Rather than buying a specially made long line, some people use a washing line tied securely to the dog's collar.

- If your Golden refuses to come when called, attach the line and keep it loose so your pup does not feel restrained. Hold the excess in your other hand.

- Sit him a short distance away and ask him to come.

- Every time he comes when called, praise and extend the line so he is further away. If he does not respond to your recall, shorten the line until he comes. Then gradually extend the length as he masters each distance.

- When your Golden comes reliably from the end of the line, you can then start training with him off the line (see above).

Never keep repeating commands. If your Golden realises that you will ask him to come a dozen times, why should he come on the first command, when he could be having so much fun with his new Labrador friend? If he does not come, run in the opposite direction. He will soon stop taking you for granted and should chase after you instantly. You can also do this if he strays too far ahead when on a walk. He will quickly realise he has to stay close and keep an eye on you – or his pathetic owner will just run off and get lost!

Sit

If your Golden is sitting, he cannot be getting into mischief, so this is a very useful command to teach early on. All pups sit – you just have to get your Golden to sit when you want him to.

To help him associate the action with the word, say "Sit" every time he sits of his own accord. Then make him feel as if he is the most intelligent dog since Lassie, praising him and giving a treat.

It won't be long before he begins to realise that putting his bottom on the floor when asked to "Sit" soon results in a treat and much adulation. Puppies are very active souls and you could be waiting all day before he sits down of his own accord. To encourage him, hold a treat above his head in such a way that when he bends his neck up and stretches to reach it, he has to put his bum on the floor. As soon as he sits, praise like mad, and give the treat he worked so hard for.

Goldens are not blonde bimbos – it won't take too long before he is reliably sitting as soon as he is asked. To make life easier and to keep your Golden mentally active, ask him to sit:

- Before feeding him
- At the kerb before crossing a road
- Before opening the front door to visitors
- Before you open the car door.

Sitting still in many of these situations could well save your dog's life. It also helps to maintain the close bond between the two of you.

When a treat is held above the puppy's head, he will naturally go into the Sit position.

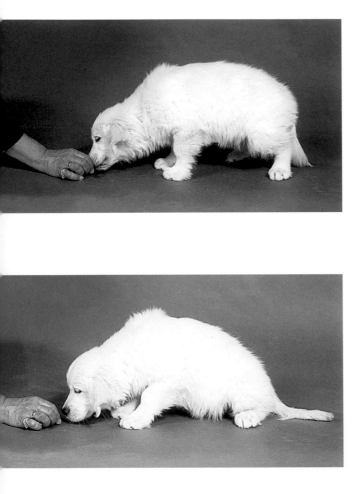

Down

As with teaching your dog to sit, say "Down" every time he lies down of his own volition. Praise and pet as enthusiastically as ever. By putting your treat-filled hand on the floor, your Golden will try every means of getting to it, and will soon realise that bending down does not quite work. Keep repeating "Down" and as soon as he drops to the floor to get closer to your hand, open your palm, give the treat and fuss him. If he simply does not understand what is expected of him, ask him to sit, then gently slide his front paws forward until he is lying down. Say "Down", and give lots of praise and a mouth-watering morsel as a reward.

As with all commands, practise throughout the day at impromptu moments – when watching TV, or in the middle of vacuuming, for example. When you feel he has mastered this command, try it when he is in the middle of a good gallop in the park. If he halts mid-flow and goes down, you know you have really cracked it.

Stay

Once your pup is reliably sitting and lying down on command, you can proceed to the "Stay" or "Wait" command. This can be difficult to teach as it is so passive, and pups like actively doing things. Staying or waiting is downright boring and purposeless as far as pups are concerned. It can be even more difficult with a Golden pup that loves being glued to your side every second of the day. Walk one step back from him, and he will very likely take one step forward – or just give it all up and run to you.

Following his nose – and the treat – a puppy will ease himself into the Down.

Build up the Stay exercise in simple stages.

The key to success is to take each step very slowly. Get your dog to sit, then say "Wait" and almost immediately give him a treat before he has a chance to move. Gradually extend the length of time between asking him to wait and giving the treat. At the end of each exercise, run up to him for a joyful reunion, or ask him to come to you for praise and a treat.

Once he has mastered this, take a step back and repeat the entire process. Then take another step back and so on. If he fails at a certain distance, take a step forward and do not move back until he will sit 100 per cent of the time. Try him lying down and waiting, as well as sitting and waiting, too.

Once he has passed this with flying colours, introduce distractions. Ask a friend to walk past your Golden while he is in a "Wait", ask someone to walk past with a dog, and so on. The more temptation he has to overcome, the bigger the praise when he has refused to succumb to it.

Collar And Lead

Wearing a collar and lead can come as a bit of a shock to a pup that has only ever worn a huge smile before now. You should get him used to collars by popping a very soft one on him for just a few minutes at a time. Make a great fuss of him when he is wearing it, so that he learns to look forward to you putting it on. It is worth

Ask your puppy to sit on your left-hand side, and make sure you have his attention.

Move off, encouraging your puppy to follow you.

removing his collar whenever you go out and leave your Golden on his own – just to prevent tragedy should he get it hooked on something and be unable to remove it.

You can start the basics of lead-training in the garden. After his vaccinations have been completed and he is taken out on a lead, it is only natural for the pup to steam ahead to investigate everything, especially so when in an exciting public place. Again, the Golden's irresistible desire to become chums with everyone in sight does not make lead-training the easiest skill to teach. It will make life immeasurably easier in the future, however, as six stones (84lb) of adult Golden Retriever will be far more difficult to cope with than a small pup. So start training while you still have a winning chance – and while your arms are both still the same length!

Again, the key to this exercise is to make your Golden really want to be with you. Before you start, get your dog's attention and make sure you maintain it throughout the walk. Use your Golden's favourite toy or treats to make sure he stays close and remains attentive.

Everyone develops their own way of on-lead walking, but these guidelines are worth following:

- Ask your dog to sit on your left-hand side. Hold the lead in your right hand, leaving your left hand free to praise, hold a toy and to give treats.
- As you set off, encourage your dog and use the command "Heel" or "Close". Talk to your dog all the time he is walking well.
- Do not fall into the trap of playing tug-of-war if he steams ahead. Pulling your Golden backwards when he strains on the leash will only encourage him to pull even more – despite the fact that it half-chokes him as a result.
- Your Golden is pulling because he wants to get somewhere quickly. If he pulls, therefore, stop. That way, he will soon realise that pulling does not get him anywhere at all.
- Ask him to come back, and position him in a sit by your side to start again. Stop and repeat every time the lead becomes taut.
- To keep him on his toes, it is worth turning off in a different direction suddenly or changing pace so he learns he has to keep alert.

As with all aspects of training, encourage all the family to get involved. Everyone in the household should be able to control the family dog. Even if one person takes main responsibility for walking duties, your Golden should still walk well for the children and other family members.

CHAPTER THREE

THE ADOLESCENT GOLDEN RETRIEVER

After surviving the trauma of puppyhood, you probably thought life would take an upturn. Well, almost... You just have to get through your dog's adolescence first. Once that is out of the way, you can sit back and be rewarded by all your hard work – and enjoy owning a fully-grown, perfectly behaved, adult Golden. Until then, you will have to cope with your dog's raging hormones and the chaos of doggie delinquency.

HORMONAL HAVOC

From the age of seven to eight months, your Golden will start leaving puppyhood behind and will be heading towards sexual maturity. This is traditionally a difficult time for owners, as a young dog often becomes more assertive, and questions his role in the family pack. This type of rebellious behaviour is more typical of dogs than bitches.

However, the Golden's generally easy-going personality comes to the rescue, and the problems encountered at this time are usually less severe than those experienced in some other breeds.

Leadership

The key to surviving the teenage phase is to maintain control and to be consistent. During adolescence, your Golden may be more willing to exploit any weaknesses you exhibit, and may try to challenge your authority unless you make it clear you are the boss. Be firm, but fair, so that he does not become confused as to his position in the household hierarchy. This is not to say that you cannot be soppy with your Golden. You can still love him and have fun with him, but do not let your discipline slip. The moment you let him get away with, for example, stealing food, you are on a slippery slope to pet anarchy. If your Golden has got away with something once, he will figure he can do it again, and again, and again...

Do not be embarrassed to sign up for a training class if you cannot solve the problems alone. Training classes are not just for puppies; they are a means of maintaining discipline and providing an opportunity for social interaction with other dogs, which will be beneficial throughout your Golden's life.

TROUBLE-SHOOTING

The Recall

Coming when called can be a real problem in the adolescent Golden Retriever. However much

There may be times when your Golden Retriever appears 'deaf' to your calls.

he loves you, it doesn't take much for him to be distracted, and to sniff out an interesting scent, or run off with some new-found friends, ignoring your desperate pleas for him to come back. Yes, he is likely to come back eventually, but you should work on having sufficient control over him that he will come back when *you* want him to, not when *he* decides to.

It won't be easy. Although usually motivated by food, the Golden is one of the few breeds that will give up a tasty treat to be in the company of humans. You might have a pocket laden with your dog's favourite biscuits, but if your Golden spots a group of children playing ball the other side of the park, even the tastiest biscuit will take second place.

Early recall training (see page 29) is essential to give you a fighting chance in your dog's adolescence. This is the age at which your Golden is likely to be more adventurous and keen to investigate everything. If you do not get on top of his recall problem, or any other disobedient behaviour, it will be even more difficult to rectify once the behaviour is established.

It is important that your Golden sees coming to you as an enjoyable experience. Think about the routine of going for a walk: you take your Golden out, let him off the lead, and he has a great time playing and running around; then you look at your watch, call him over, he comes, you put him on the lead, and you take him home. Your Golden is an intelligent dog, and it won't take him long to work out that every time you call him over, the fun ends and he is taken home. By refusing to come, he prolongs his time outside; and, if you start chasing him around to put him on the lead, this game becomes even more exciting.

When out on a walk, keep calling your Golden over and give him a treat. Then send him off to play again. Never put the lead on immediately after calling him. If that doesn't work, take your Golden's bowl and breakfast out with you. Serve it just before returning home, and he is likely to be persuaded back. This will also help him to regard coming back as a rewarding experience. Repeat for his evening walk.

Jumping Up

Goldens are renowned for jumping up. This is not a problem when your dog is a small bundle of fluff, but when he is an adolescent – with the mind of a pup but the body of an adult – it is a nuisance. As well as getting muddy paws and scratch marks on your clothes and arms, it can also be dangerous, especially if your dog knocks over a young child or an elderly person.

Jumping up is a behaviour your Golden probably learnt as a puppy: when people came into the house, he received lots of affection. He would have grown up believing all visitors came only to see him, and so would seek attention if it was not immediately given. If he stretched up to a visitor, he may have received even more fuss, as he would have looked so cute doing it.

The Golden's love of people is at the heart of this problem: he just loves them so much, he wants to get as close as possible. This is also the

Jumping up may be endearing in a small puppy, but it can be positively dangerous in an adult dog.

key to solving the inappropriate behaviour. Because Goldens thrive on human attention, you should withhold it if he jumps up. Do not look at him, touch him or speak to him, just completely ignore him. That way, he will soon realise that jumping up is counterproductive. The minute his paws go back on the floor, however, you should shower him with praise, pats and kisses.

Aggression

'Aggression' and 'Goldens' are not two words that are usually uttered in the same breath. By nature, Goldens are gentle-natured dogs, and aggression resulting from hormone-induced dominance is quite rare.

Aggression With Other Dogs

Although nature gives the Golden an affable temperament, nurture still plays a part. If a Golden is not properly socialised, problems can quickly develop – particularly with dog-to-dog aggression. A dog that is not properly socialised may display nervous aggression because he has not had the opportunity to realise that other dogs should be viewed as potential playmates, rather than constituting a threat. He needs to learn how to interpret doggie language, and to respond accordingly.

The principle behind nervous aggression is that attack is the best form of defence. It only takes one bad experience to confirm the dog's suspicions that unfamiliar dogs are a threat. It can be difficult to rehabilitate your dog after an attack, as your own feelings may reinforce your Golden's fears. For example, if your Golden is attacked by a particular type of dog, you are more likely to behave nervously next time you encounter a similar dog. Your Golden will pick up on your unease, and will believe that there *is*

Goldens are rarely aggressive with other dogs.

something to fear, and his nervous aggression will increase. It is a catch-22 situation.

Obviously you will be concerned if you fear that your Golden will be attacked by other dogs, and you may well be embarrassed if your dog appears to be a bully, but it is important to be as relaxed as possible when encountering dogs on your daily walks. Being so closely bonded to their owners and their moods, Goldens can interpret even the most subtle body language – a slight tightening of the lead for instance. Although it can be difficult to stand back and let the dogs get on with it, it is often the best solution.

Dogs have great communication skills, and they will soon sort out their own hierarchy. A dog kept on a short lead is more likely to feel intimidated by other dogs, as he is not free to check them out, have a sniff, and say 'hello' in the usual way. With smaller breeds, such as the Yorkshire Terrier, an owner's fear is more understandable, as tiny dogs can be hurt accidentally; but the Golden Retriever is robust enough to enjoy some friendly rough-and-tumble and come out unscathed.

Aggression With People

Goldens are 'people dogs' – they love sharing their lives with their human families, and aggression towards their two-legged friends is rare. However, as with any breed, Goldens who are bred by irresponsible breeders for money rather than to improve the breed, can be sub-

'Introduce your Golden to positive experiences with people'

standard in temperament, as well as in health. Those that are poorly socialised with people can also develop fear-aggression towards them.

The key is to prevent aggression in the first place. Having bought your Golden puppy from a reputable breeder, you should get him used to being handled by a variety of people – young and old. Persuade all family members to do the exercises outlined in Chapter Two, that teach the pup to develop good bite inhibition, and train him to accept his collar and food-bowl being touched. Introducing your Golden to as many positive experiences with people as possible should ensure he grows up with no hang-ups.

One of the most common forms of aggression in the home is caused by an obsessive guarding behaviour of food, toys and other possessions. This can have insecurity, or even dominance, at its root. Whatever the cause, you should consult a qualified animal behaviourist at once for expert advice and treatment. Your vet should be able to refer you to someone suitable.

Separation Anxiety

It is important that the adolescent Golden receives plenty of mental stimulation to keep his mind occupied. No dog should be isolated for long periods, as he is bound to get into mischief. Neglect can also lead to behavioural problems, such as separation anxiety. Who can blame a dog for ripping up the sofa if he is left at home alone from 8am to 6pm every day

Your dog must develop the confidence to be left alone without experiencing undue anxiety.

while the owner is out at work? Dogs should never be left alone all day. Owners who work full-time, should make the necessary care arrangements, perhaps organising for a neighbour to dog-sit, or employing a dog-walker.

Separation anxiety can also be caused by a very different situation – by being with a dog all day, every day. This is more likely to affect owners who do not work, or who work at home. After a Golden has become accustomed to having his owners around all the time, even being left at home for 20 minutes can be traumatic for him. He may express his feelings of insecurity by barking incessantly to call his owners back, scrabbling at the door to get to them, or becoming destructive in his attempts to relieve his anxiety.

However much your Golden loves being with you, and you with him, it is important to recognise the importance of having time apart. This does not just mean being in different rooms, or leaving your dog in the house for brief spells; you should also set up a system of

non-contact between you when you are both together. This means that your Golden should recognise that you give him attention when *you* are ready, not because *he* demands it.

Some behaviourists recommend having a visual signal – such as a towel hanging on the door handle – which indicates that a period of 'time-out' will follow. Whenever the signal is in use, you should ignore the dog, so that he recognises what it signifies. Initially, use your signal for just a few minutes, and gradually prolong the period of time, until your Golden can happily last half an hour without having any contact with you. When you progress to leaving your dog in the house for a short period, displaying your signal a few minutes before you go should lessen the dog's anxiety, as he will have learned not to expect any contact anyway. When you leave the house, do not make a big fuss over saying good-bye – this will only exacerbate the problem.

A separation problem should not be ignored, as it can cause great distress to your dog. If the condition continues, you should consult a pet behaviourist.

Getting The Hump

There will be many times in the next few years when your dog causes you embarrassment, and this will be one of them. As soon as a male hits sexual maturity, he may start 'humping'. Cushions, legs, the cat... nothing will be safe. And you can guarantee that he will feel the urge whenever you have visitors around.

Although it may initially have a hormonal

cause, this type of behaviour can become habitual – even after the dog has been neutered – so be sure to stop your Golden as soon as you see him doing it.

Humping isn't just about sex, it can also be about dominance over another, so do not be surprised if your bitch starts exhibiting this behaviour, too.

NEUTERING

If you do not intend to breed from your Golden Retriever, it is worth considering the option of neutering. This is not only a means of countering some behavioural problems, there are important health considerations. Spaying a bitch dramatically reduces her chances of mammary tumours and removes her future risk of pyometra. In a dog, castration prevents testicular cancer and markedly reduces the chance of prostate disorders.

There are some disadvantages to neutering. There can be a tendency to put on weight, though dietary control can keep this in check. Coat changes may also occur, and some Goldens can develop a woolly coat – particularly over the back and hindquarters. Incontinence in bitches can occur very occasionally.

As well as considering the health implications, there is also the question of convenience. Could you cope with a bitch coming into season twice a year, and each time ensuring she is kept away from all other dogs for about 21 days? Could you cope with an errant dog who disappears for days on end in pursuit of the scent of a bitch on heat?

At what age your Golden is neutered will very much depend on your vet. Some firmly believe that it should be done after sexual maturity – at about six months for a dog, and after her first season for a bitch. Others find it preferable to neuter sooner, in some cases as early as 18-20 weeks.

If, having examined the pros and cons, you are still unsure about what is best for your own dog, talk to your vet.

If you are not planning to breed from your Golden Retriever, it is sensible to consider the option of neutering.

CHAPTER FOUR

THE FAMILY DOG

The Golden Retriever is the ultimate family pet. Unlike some breeds, he is not a 'one-man dog', and will love all family members equally. Intelligent and eager to please, this is a dog that responds to training and thrives on mental stimulation.

HAPPY FAMILIES

A Golden Retriever makes an enthusiastic addition to most families. He loves being invited to any family event – barbecues, parties and trips out – and may be quite offended if he is excluded. If your dog is well-behaved, there is no reason why he should not share as much of your life as possible. In fact, he will find a place in your affections so quickly, that family activities will seem very incomplete without him.

When not engaged in a family activity, a Golden likes to find his own amusement. Picking up something left lying around and carrying it around in his mouth is a particular favourite. If you can't find your hat, gloves, or socks, you can bet your dog has the now soggy items hidden in his bed. Having a Golden in the house, who is constantly on the search for the canine equivalent of a dummy or comfort blanket, will soon teach all family members to be tidy – even teenagers!

When you see your Golden taking something that isn't his, tell him "No" firmly and give him one of his own toys. However, the temptation to have something 'forbidden' may be just too much for him, so the general rule is: if you don't want it covered in dog slobber, keep it out of reach.

SECOND-HAND DOGS

There are those who feel they would like to offer an adult rescued dog a home. Yes, puppies are fun, but they are not for everyone. Perhaps you do not relish life in the fast lane, racing after a pup who is heading, at lightning speed,

GOLDEN CHILD

Introducing a puppy to a household with children needs careful planning (see Chapter Two), but extra thought needs to be given when bringing a baby into the home of established Goldens. Kathy Donaldson already had three Golden Retrievers when she had the first of her two children.

"I think having three Goldens probably helped as they were used to having to wait for attention. If you have one dog, it can sometimes become the focus of attention all the time.

"I let the dogs sniff each baby when they were brought home, and they quickly seemed to recognise them as their family. Even now, if there is a blond-haired boy in the street, one of the dogs, Teal, will put her nose in the air to sniff if it is 'hers'.

"I made sure the dogs were never excluded. But, at the same time, they had to know the boundaries – such as not picking up the children's toys. If they did, I just said "No" and took the toy away and gave them one of their own. It didn't take them long to learn. Now, if there is a pile of children's and dogs' toys, the dogs will sniff out which ones they can touch.

"I also make sure the dogs have a safe haven. They go to their beds if they need peace and quiet, and the children have been taught to respect that.

"There haven't been any problems at all. Goldens just want to be in the middle of family chaos all the time. Far from tolerating it, they seem to revel in it."

The Golden Retriever loves being part of family life.

for your priceless antique vase. A recently retired couple, who now have time to devote to a dog, could be ideal.

However, if you see a rescued dog as a cheap way of getting hold of a pedigree, forget it. The initial outlay may be less, but you must still be prepared to pay for food, toys, bedding, vet's bills, and possibly even behaviourist's bills if your dog has particular problems.

Goldens, like most breeds, are usually in rescue through no fault of their own. Marriage break-ups are often responsible – where both partners move out and have to work to support themselves, leaving no-one at home to look after the dog. Many dogs end up in rescue when their elderly owners can no longer cope on their own and move into residential accommodation or sheltered housing – and the invitation may not

TO THE RESCUE

Lynn Newton and her husband, Mark, took on Josh, a young neutered Golden Retriever, from rescue kennels about 16 months ago. He is their first rescue; they are his third home.

"When we brought him home, he treated the whole experience as great fun and a big adventure. He was extremely boisterous, confident and ready to take advantage of anything and everything. Because he lacked discipline, we had to begin as with a new puppy, and teach him some house rules and basic manners!

"Because of his outgoing, confident nature, we assumed Josh was okay and expected him to settle much too quickly. However, after a couple of weeks, the 'holiday' period was over for him – maybe he realised that he was not about to go home after an adventure. His behaviour became more unpredictable towards people. Some friends found him moody, he would elicit attention and then suddenly change his mind and growl and snap, and would completely ignore other visitors to the house. He even bit my uncle quite badly – without any warning signs.

It took Josh some time to feel secure and loved in his new home.

"Josh becomes suspicious of people if they call him over to make a fuss of him. He is even threatened if people simply talk to him, and is likely to become edgy and snap. We now tell guests to ignore Josh completely – he will go over to them to sniff and say 'hello' if he wants to.

"It is a good idea for the dog to have a place of his very own. For Josh, this is his bed. He has one in the kitchen and one in our bedroom. If we tell him to go to his bed when anyone visits, he knows he is safe and will not be touched or spoken to. When he feels like it, he will come out and say 'hello', often going straight back to bed again.

"We also send him to bed when we eat, as he is quite possessive around food, and more likely to snap. We were advised to give him three meals a day to help with his obsession (it reduces the significance of just one main feed and creates a routine, to stop him expecting food outside his meal-times).

"Because I am with him all day, Josh became increasingly possessive of me, and always lies down next to me if other people are around. He is basically very insecure underneath the bluster and needs to be constantly reassured by me touching him. Whereas, in his first few weeks, he was willing to accept and welcome anyone, now he is more cautious. He has found his pack and his security and seems afraid that other people may threaten it. Maybe this is because he has such an unsettled past and doesn't want to be moved again.

"My advice to anyone taking on a rescue Golden would be to allow him plenty of time and space. You can't explain to the dog what is happening, so you just have to wait while the new situation gradually becomes familiar, routine and secure.

"Dogs love routine and security. Our previous Retriever, Holly, which we had owned since she was six weeks old until her death at 10 years, took both for granted. Josh doesn't take anything for granted. Whenever I leave him for even a short time, he greets me as if we have been apart for weeks. Every morning, he races upstairs to wake me, and won't stay in the garden for very long before rushing in to 'touch base'.

"Taking on an adult dog as his third home is a big commitment, fraught with more problems than we naively anticipated. It is totally different from buying a six-week Retriever pup and bringing it up and training it yourself. We feel as if we adopted Josh during his adolescence, whereas Holly was ours from the beginning.

"Time, love, patience and understanding are very important when taking on a rescue. You have to try to see things from the dog's point of view. You are taking on a completely unknown quantity. You don't know what has happened in the dog's past, and you try to latch on to any signs or indications to give you some clues.

"Having Josh to live with us has been trying and worrying at times, but very rewarding. We love him very, very much and are looking forward to many happy years together."

necessarily extend to the dog. These Goldens, who have already known love and fitted in with family life usually adapt quickly to a new home.

Many 'problem' Goldens that come in for rehoming are puppy-farmed (puppy-milled) dogs that have been sold indiscriminately to inappropriate homes, without advice to owners of the time and commitment involved. Money is the name of the game, and the popular Golden Retriever is always at risk from this type of exploitation. The puppies in these establishments are usually raised in kennels and have little human contact. As a result of this lack of socialisation, they often face tremendous problems coping with family life. Other behavioural problems with puppy-farmed dogs in rescue may be the result of indiscriminate breeding, with no care being taken to choose the best examples of the breed, both temperamentally and physically.

Puppies are sometimes available from rescue, though they are usually snapped up quite quickly. Many 'problem' dogs come into rescue aged about 18 months, during the difficult adolescent stage (see Chapter Three).

This is not to say that you should dismiss a rescue Golden. Nurture wins hands down over nature, and many behavioural problems can be overcome with careful handling and infinite love and patience. As a breed, the Golden adapts well to a new home – his soft spot for people helps him through the loss of his former family. Most owners find their rescued Golden settles very quickly – and the organisation will get a call a

'A rescued Golden needs time to rebuild confidence'

couple of weeks later saying the dog has adapted so well, that he is behaving as if he has always lived there.

The high rehoming success of rescue organisations is a result of their hard work at matching the individual dog to a suitable family. Contrary to popular belief, it is not usually a case of first-come first-served – more waiting for the 'right dog' to come up for adoption.

It is often said that a puppy is like a blank sheet of paper – he becomes whatever you make him. If you put in the love and hard work, you should end up with a dog you can be proud of. The opposite is true of a rescued dog, and you must be prepared to spend a considerable amount of time correcting bad habits before starting work on a new training regime. But the rewards are great, and in the vast majority of cases, a rescued Golden just needs understanding, and time to rebuild his confidence in humans.

CARING FOR THE ADULT GOLDEN

After spending considerable time and energy training and socialising your puppy, you can relax a little more now you have an adult dog. However, it is important to remember that training must be maintained, so all your hard work does not get forgotten. With regard to caring for your adult Golden, the priorities are:

- Feeding
- Exercise
- Grooming

- Mental stimulation... and heaps and heaps of love.

Feeding Needs

Food is a Golden's chief pleasure. They are rarely fussy eaters and will usually wolf down whatever is placed in front of them .

Some owners feed once a day, others twice a day. This is largely a matter of personal convenience, but whatever you decide, you must stick to a routine. If your Golden never knows when his next meal is coming, he will be in a constant state of anticipation, and will become a nuisance, begging every time food is produced.

There are many dog foods on the market, but do not be

Mealtime – the high spot of a Golden Retriever's day!

tempted to keep chopping and changing. Dogs are not like humans, and they do not appreciate a different food for every meal. The breeder will have recommended a diet from puppyhood to adulthood, and it is safest to stick with this, unless problems occur. If your Golden does not seem to be thriving, consult your vet. Most practices now take an active interest in nutrition, and will give expert advice on the different types of food available, and the correct quantities to feed.

If you need to change your Golden's diet, add a little of the new food at each meal. Gradually increase the amount until, eventually, you have completed a changeover. The veteran Golden may have special needs (see 'Golden Oldies', Page 56).

Weight

There is a significant difference in size between male and female Golden Retrievers, and, obviously, there is also size variation among dogs of the same sex. However, as a general rule, the average weight of an adult Golden male in top-class condition is about 75 lbs, and a bitch about 65 lbs.

It can be difficult to resist those big doleful Golden eyes, but do not give in. Over-feeding soon causes obesity, which puts undue pressure on the heart and joints. Not only will the quality of your dog's life be affected, but you could actually put his life at risk. Do not kill your dog with kindness – there are more ways to a Golden's heart than through his stomach. A game with his favourite toy is just as rewarding – and far healthier.

Exercise

After years of being bred to be active, the modern dog does not take kindly to a couch-

FUN AND GAMES

Golden Retrievers were bred for an active life, and one of the joys of owning this breed is to see them enjoying themselves – on land and in water.

potato lifestyle. You might be able to switch the TV off with a remote control, and order a pizza just by picking up the phone, but a dog – especially a breed as energetic as the Golden Retriever – does not thrive on indolence.

Goldens were bred to spend long days retrieving game over land and in water, often in harsh weather conditions. Although the working instinct has been partially diluted in some non-working strains, it is still an integral part of the breed. A Golden Retriever needs to keep busy – both mentally and physically. If all you can manage is a quick trot down the road once a day, you are better off owning a smaller, less demanding breed. A bored dog is a often a destructive dog – and you only have yourself to blame if this situation arises.

The minimum exercise for an adult Golden is half an hour in the morning and in the evening. A puppy's exercise requirements are not as excessive (see Chapter Two), but an adult dog needs at least an hour every day – in all weathers, on high days and holidays, for the rest of his life. A Golden does not understand the concept of a Sunday morning lie-in – and by the time you have owned a dog for a few years, neither will you!

It only takes a whiff of a wood or a field and the Golden's natural desire to investigate kicks into action. He will think nothing of diving through brambles on the trail of an interesting scent. To avoid accidents, remove your dog's collar when allowing him to run free as it might

' Retrieving stimulates both mind and body '

get caught on a branch. Make sure your dog is also microchipped or tattooed, as he will have no other form of identification once his collar is removed.

As well as free-running, road work (on-lead walking on a hard pavement) is also important. It helps to keep the pads hard and the nails short, as well as improving muscle tone. Swimming is a great favourite with most Goldens. Make sure you choose a safe place, where there are no strong currents, and where there is easy access in and out of the water. This form of exercise is especially good for older dogs as it will build up the muscle without putting strain on the joints. However, make sure your Golden does not swim in cold water for too long and does not over-exert himself, or you could do more harm than good.

Retrieving is in the Golden's genes – and is a great way of keeping him mentally and physically active. Make sure you throw safe toys for him to fetch – sticks and balls that are small enough to be swallowed are strictly out of bounds. Most pet shops stock specially designed retrieving toys, such as tough rubber rings and floating toys on a rope for water retrieval.

With the chewing stage safely in their puppy past, most adult Goldens are very soft-mouthed. Orally fixated they may be, never happier than when walking round with something in their mouth, but they are unlikely to destroy anything. In fact, a healthy, happy Golden that has plenty of mental and physical exercise is less likely to be destructive than most other breeds.

Town Versus Country

The Golden will adapt to either town or country life. Some cities – London and New York being prime examples – actually have more public open space than areas of the countryside that are under intensive cultivation, so it is perfectly viable to raise a healthy dog in an urban environment.

Obviously, your Golden will enjoy life in the country, and there may be some wonderful opportunities for free-running. But the countryside is not necessarily a trouble-free idyll. For example, road-walking your Golden along unlit, winding country lanes (with no pavements/side-walks) can be dangerous. You must also make sure your dog is absolutely safe with sheep and any other animals he may encounter. Do not take any chances – always put your dog on a lead if he is around sheep.

Wherever you live, never leave home without a suitable bag or two so you can always pick up after your dog.

Digging

Goldens love digging – it is virtually impossible to stop them doing it, so don't waste your breath. Instead, allocate a place in your garden where your dog *can* dig without ruining your plants or tunnelling under the fence. Teach your Golden to understand what is allowed by encouraging him to dig in the chosen spot, and rewarding him for digging there. Give a firm "No" if he ventures into non-digging territory.

You might even consider putting a sand pit in your garden which will provide ready-made entertainment.

Most Goldens enjoy being groomed.

Grooming

Goldens have a glorious coat, and brushing your dog every day should not be seen as a chore. Most dogs enjoy the attention, and it helps to strengthen the bond between you. It also provides an opportunity to keep a close check on your dog, so you spot any signs of trouble at an early stage.

Groom with the same comb and brush you have been using during your Golden's puppyhood (see Chapter Two). If your dog is attended to daily, it should take no more than 10 minutes at most. The task only becomes more arduous if you leave it for a week at a time, allowing mats and tangles to form.

Goldens are great explorers, and it is easy to pick up burrs in the undergrowth. These will need to be removed by teasing them out gently with a comb. Be extra vigilant for seasonal grass seeds in the coat, around the eyes and ears and between the pads. The seeds can penetrate under the skin, causing severe problems, if they are not removed.

Mud can be removed fairly easily by letting it dry and then brushing it out. If your Golden has found something delightful to roll in and a bath is crucial, give him a brush-through first and then put him in the bath or shower cubicle.

Work through the coat thoroughly, making sure you have got down to the under-coat.

Bath Time

- Always use a rubber mat, so that your dog does not slip.
- Make sure you use a specially manufactured dog shampoo (other types of shampoo or detergent could set up a skin allergy).
- The water should be lukewarm, and it is easiest if this is applied with a shower appliance.
- After shampooing your dog, rinse thoroughly to ensure that all traces of soap have been removed.
- Give him a good rub down with a towel to remove the excess water.
- Use a hairdryer (on moderate heat) and groom as you dry.

Brush Up

Remember that the Golden has a doublecoat. Using an inappropriate flat brush may groom the surface top-coat a treat but leave the under-wool matted. As you are grooming, you should be able to feel whether you have got to the bottom of the under-coat. If you cannot tell, examine the coat.

- Always groom from the head downwards so that you work in a logical order and do not forget any areas.
- Start at the top of the head and work down to the neck, checking behind the ears for any lumps of matted coat.
- Work down the neck to the shoulders, to the elbows and legs. Mats are often found under the arms, and these will need to be combed out
- Check between the paws where hair often grows in clumps. This may need to be trimmed if it becomes excessive.
- Groom the belly, working up through the ribcage, and up to the back.
- Work on the trousers and finish with the tail. As a continuation of the spine, the tail is a particularly sensitive part of the dog's body, so be very gentle.

- Much of the undercoat moults in warmer weather, so regular grooming, to remove the dead hair, is especially important at this time.

In Trim

If a Golden Retriever is being exhibited in the show ring, he will need special preparation in order to show himself to full advantage. Show dogs are trimmed, and it is worth watching a professional groomer to see what should be done. The main principle is to work in harmony with the natural shape of the dog. The dog's appearance should be subtly enhanced – not altered in any major way.

- The feet are trimmed to show their natural size and contour.
- The tail should reach the hocks (the joint in each hind-leg which points behind the dog like a reverse knee). The tail is trimmed to the correct length, and then shaped in a gradual fan-like curve.
- Check all areas where feathering grows, including the ears, to ensure they are neat and tidy. Some Goldens have much more feathering than others, and they will need more work.

Routine Care

Your Golden should be used to routine handling so that you can check him over at least once a week (see Chapter Two). Firstly, examine the dog all over, feeling for any lumps or bumps that should not be there.

Ears

The Golden's ears are not erect, so air cannot easily circulate in them. They are therefore prone to infections and mites. Purchase a suitable ear-cleaner from your vet and follow the instructions carefully. Never push cotton buds into the ear. At best, you are likely to push dirt *into* the ear rather than removing it; at worst, you can cause serious damage to the ear.

Nails

It is important not to allow the nails to grow too long as this can cause discomfort, leading to lameness. In most cases, nails will wear down naturally – long nails may indicate the dog is not having enough road-walking exercise. If necessary, trim the nails with guillotine nail-clippers.

Nails may need clipping if your dog is not getting enough exercise on hard surfaces.

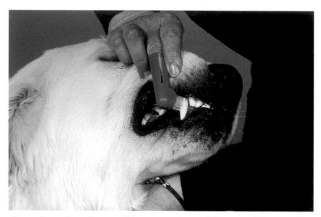

Regular cleaning will prevent problems with teeth and gums.

Dental Care

Dogs rarely get tooth decay. However, if tartar builds it can cause painful gum disease, which, left unchecked, can lead to teeth falling out. A weekly brushing with a toothbrush or finger brush (all from good pet stores) should prevent problems. Meaty-flavoured toothpaste for dogs is available to make the experience more enjoyable.

If you feed tinned food, make sure biscuits are added. Giving your dog dental chews or rope toys to chew on also helps to remove tartar.

GOLDEN OLDIES

By the time your Golden has reached old age, he is a mellow, beautifully behaved animal. For many, this is a very special time. You have both grown to know each other inside out, and there is a very close loving bond between you. Your Golden knows your house rules (through years of you consistently upholding them), and he knows exactly what you will, and will not, tolerate. Your Golden will give you loyal companionship, and, in return, you should provide all the home comforts.

This 'retirement' period is far easier than the hectic early years. However, there are special considerations when looking after an older dog. The veteran generally needs more sleep and a slower pace of life. He can become less tolerant, so if you have younger dogs, make sure your oldie gets periods of peace and quiet away from them.

Let your dog dictate how much exercise he needs. Some Goldens remain as active and energetic as ever, but the vast majority require less exercise. There are some dogs who desperately try to keep up – to the detriment of their health – so it is important to be aware of individual needs.

Always dry your Golden thoroughly when you return from a walk. He should not be left cold and wet for any length of time; as well as being uncomfortable to him, it may also affect his joints. Remember that if your Golden is taking less exercise, his nails may need trimming more often.

As your dog's senses become less acute, his appetite may suffer. Many animals rely on their sense of smell to whet their appetite, and if this is dulled, it may result in a lack of interest in food. Warming moist food slightly often releases its smell and will therefore make it more appetising. There are also many special complete-food veteran diets available which cater for your dog's changing dietary needs.

Gum disease and teeth decay can also contribute to a lack of enjoyment in food. If you have maintained regular oral hygiene

Diet and exercise will need to be regulated as your dog grows older.

throughout the dog's life, the problem is less likely to arise. But if you suspect teeth trouble, ask your vet to make a thorough examination.

Euthanasia

Allowing your much-loved Golden to die peacefully and in dignity is one of the greatest responsibilities you have as a pet owner. It is also the most difficult. It is a time for being absolutely selfless: although losing your dog may be very painful, you must consider his well-being above everything else.

Once the vet can do no more, and your Golden's quality of life has deteriorated, it may be kinder to put him to sleep. You should be guided by your vet as to the prognosis, but ultimately the decision is yours. Having spent many years sharing your life with your Golden, only you can know when the right time comes.

There are a variety of options available to you to suit your individual needs and preferences. If your dog gets stressed going to the vet, you might like to arrange a home-visit so your Golden dies peacefully in familiar surroundings. Some people like to bury their pets in the garden. Others opt to have them cremated, either keeping the ashes in a box or casket, or choosing to scatter them on the dog's favourite walk.

All pet owners suffer the distress of losing their animals. If you find it particularly difficult and need someone to talk to, ask your vet for details of your nearest pet bereavement counsellor. If one isn't available, a general counsellor may be able to help you come to terms with your loss.

SAYING GOODBYE

Losing a dog is never easy, as Brenda and John Taylor discovered when their first dog, Mac, had to be put to sleep.

"When you get a dog, you know it's not going to be with you for ever, but you expect it to have a certain life-span. We knew quite early on that Mac wouldn't have as long as other dogs, and that was like a shadow over us for several years.

"When he was a puppy, Mac ran down a hill and collided with Sherrie, my older Golden. He hurt his shins so we took him to the vet. While being X-rayed, the vet saw he had slight hip dysplasia and told us Mac would be prone to arthritis in later life. At four years, X-rays showed the arthritis had taken hold, and 18 months later, it had got worse. By the age of seven, it had become severe.

"We had tried various treatments and medications over the years, and finally there was nothing else left to ease his pain; we had explored every avenue.

"It's always difficult choosing the right-time. In the morning, Mac would seem fine on our walks, but he would get slower and slower, and by the time we returned home, he was clearly in pain. Yes, he could have gone on for a bit longer, but it wasn't right. He was in pain and he didn't have a good quality of life. Other dogs may not mind spending their lives sleeping on the sofa, but Golden Retrievers – and Mac in particular – really loved long walks, and he just couldn't do it any more. Some days, he couldn't move at all.

"We gave Mac a lovely walk before taking him to the vet to be put to sleep. After that, we drove him to an animal crematorium. We didn't want anyone else touching him and wanted to know exactly what was going to happen to him. His ashes are still on our sideboard.

"I don't think losing a dog will ever be that bad again. It was awful. Even a couple of months later, I had dreadful depression. I thought I would be okay because I had been prepared for it, but it took a very long time. People with single dogs have their whole routines changed when their dog dies, but I still had three at home, so I was still going for our regular walks. But there was a huge void. The other dogs are special, and they have their own place in my heart – and Mac had his, which can't be filled by anyone else.

"Despite the grief, the relief that he was at rest and out of pain was immense. You have to be very brave and put your own feelings aside completely – in favour of the dog's needs. With Sherrie, my 15-year-old Golden, I just hope she dies peacefully in her sleep. But whatever age they die, old or young, it is always painful. With a young dog, you feel robbed, as if they haven't had their time, but with older dogs you miss them because they've been around so long. It's never easy.

"But time is relative. However old your dog is, if you can say they have had a really good life, then you cannot reproach yourself for making the decision to put them to sleep. It's the quality, not the quantity, of life that counts."

CHAPTER FIVE

BROADENING HORIZONS

The aim of every owner is to have a well-behaved, adaptable dog, and if you have worked hard training and socialising your puppy during the first year of his life, you should have achieved this goal. For some, this is enough, and, although it is essential to provide mental stimulation for your dog, there is no need to get involved in more advanced training. However, there is no doubt that a Golden Retriever loves the challenge of learning new things, and working with your dog increases the bond between you.

There are a variety of different canine activities available, and the discipline you choose is largely a matter of personal preference – the Golden Retriever is prepared to have a go at anything!

LEARNING CITIZENSHIP

The 'Good Citizen' scheme is an excellent starting point if you want to take your Golden's training a stage further. The American Kennel Club's Canine Good Citizen Program and the British Kennel Club's Good Citizen Dog Scheme encourage responsible pet ownership and educate dog owners about the benefits of having a well-behaved pet.

Early training and socialisation should mean that the exercises for each scheme are second-nature to your Golden. Basically, the dog must behave in a calm, confident manner in a variety of different situations. They include:

- Walking on a loose lead in a controlled manner
- Walking through a crowd
- Being approached and petted by a stranger
- Meeting another dog
- Being handled and groomed
- Responding to a number of basic commands.

ANGLO-AMERICAN DIFFERENCES

There are some variations in the obedience exercises performed in the UK and the US. A closer, tighter position is required in UK heelwork, for example.

However, the skills used in the various classes are the same (heelwork, scenting, retrieves and stays); it is just the detail which varies.

If a refresher course is needed on the basics, see Chapter Two. There are many participating training clubs in the UK and the US that offer courses to prepare your dog for the tests. To find out more information on the schemes, contact your national Kennel Club.

COMPETITIVE OBEDIENCE

Goldens enjoy any activity that involves interacting with their owners, and Competitive Obedience is no exception. They might not be as fast or as quick-witted as the Border Collie or working sheepdog (for whom Obedience could have been invented), but Goldens are probably easier to train because they are so biddable. They can also provide the collie with some stiff competition – they just have to work a little harder to achieve success.

In the UK, there have been several Golden Retriever Obedience Champions and they are one of the most popular breeds in the sport, perhaps even challenging the German Shepherd Dog for second place after the collie. In the United States, the Golden Retriever dominates the ring, with the Border Collie lagging behind. The AKC Obedience Champion title was first available in 1977. The initial three Obedience Champions were all Golden Retrievers, the very

first being a bitch (Ch. Moreland's Golden Tonka).

When looking for a Competitive Obedience competitor, it has been found that working lines can be more suitable than show lines because

Lynn Heidinger from Illinois has been training dogs in Obedience since 1967. Her third Golden, Toastie, won the AKC Obedience Invitational National Championships, which had the 100 top dogs from all over America competing.

the dogs generally have a lighter build, and some say they are more keen to learn. However, dogs from strong working lines can be a little too independent, so many successful competitors are working-show crosses.

The KC and AKC does not allow dogs under six months to compete in Obedience. However, Goldens are often late-developers, and many are over one year old before they are ready for more advanced training. This does not mean that you cannot make a start while your Golden is growing up. Competitive Obedience is a natural progression from the puppy's early training (see Chapter Two), so you can start teaching the basics, and then fine-tune as he matures.

Even when fully mature, it is important to remember that Golden Retrievers have a very low boredom threshold. To maintain concentration, keep training sessions short and frequent, and make them as much fun as possible. Goldens can also be stubborn – if they don't want to do something, they won't. The key is to motivate your dog so that he really wants to perform an exercise. Make a game of everything – a strict training session just will not work.

To find your nearest Obedience class, contact your national Kennel Club or nearest vet surgery.

Heelwork

Competitive heelwork does not come naturally to the Golden Retriever. Heavier in build, a

'Top-class heelwork takes a lot of practice'

Golden is not as agile and sure-footed as a collie, nor is he so quick to respond to his owner's movements. However, a Golden loves being glued to his owner's side, so it is usually an exercise that most will dogs enjoy and are willing to learn.

Your Golden should walk on your left side in a happy, confident manner, both on and off the lead. He should neither be ahead nor behind, but should have his head about level with your knee. He should remain consistently close if you change direction or turn around.

Exercise One

- The first step to teaching the perfect heelwork position is to practise it standing still. Stand your Golden on your left-hand side, put him in the correct position (see above) and hold a treat or a toy in your right hand, so that he learns to look at your hand. A command such as "Watch" can be used.

- As the dog gets older and bigger, you can lift your hand up closer to your face. Eventually, you can dispense with the treat and toy altogether and the dog will look at your face instead.

- Reward your Golden with a treat or a play with a toy when he stands correctly, and gradually extend the length of time he has to stand and be attentive.

Exercise Two

- Hold a treat or a toy in your right hand. With your dog on your left side, walk in a left-hand circle. Because you are walking in one direction (left), but the dog is looking in the other direction (right), you are more likely to achieve a closer heel – with the dog a little across your leg. Praise and treat whenever he is in the required position.

- Only when your Golden is walking perfectly in this way should you progress to walking a right-hand circle. Hold the treat in the same way and work on keeping the dog close to your leg. This is a more difficult exercise as you cannot guide or nudge the dog into position because he is now on the outside of the circle you are walking and you are on the inside.

- Only when it is second nature to your dog to walk close to your side can you progress on to turning and changing direction.

Retrievers

Retrievers retrieve, so this is one area where a Golden has the advantage. However, speed and precision are crucial, too.

Teaching The Exercise

- You can start to teach your Golden to retrieve from about eight weeks of age. Throw a soft toy or ball of crumpled paper and ask him to fetch it.

- Goldens have an in-built need to carry things in their mouths, so you won't have to wait long before the thrown item is in his jaws. As soon as it is, call him to you enthusiastically.

- When he comes, throw the item immediately and again ask him to fetch it. This way, he'll realise that the game does not stop when he brings the item to you – in fact, the sooner he brings it, the sooner a new game starts.

- Once he is happily retrieving soft items, you can start introducing the harder dumb-bell.

Teaching Steadiness

'Steadiness' is crucial. Your Golden has to learn to wait for the retrieve command.

- Tell him to wait, and then throw the item.

- Let him wait for just a couple of seconds

The Retrieve comes naturally – it is just a matter of curbing exuberance.

YOU CAN DU IT

Debby Quigley has trained a couple of Obedience Champions – one a Border Collie, the other a Golden Retriever – so she is perfectly placed to discuss the qualities that Goldens can offer to the sport.

"A number of years ago I had the pleasure of watching what I still think is the greatest Obedience dog I have ever seen: a Golden Retriever named Bomber. At that moment, I decided that I must have a Golden – not just any Golden, but a son of that great dog. And so it began with my first Golden called Du, otherwise known as OTCH Shoreland's Kandu Too UDX TD JH.

Debby Quigley with OTCH Shoreland's Kandu Too UDX, TD, JH.

"Du, a Bomber son, came off the plane running, playing and enjoying life. As a young puppy, he was into everything and wanted to DO everything, which is how he earned his name. However, for the first six months of his life, his name was Don't instead of Du. The minute he came into my house, we started his Obedience training mostly out of necessity and survival.

"Being the precocious Golden that he was, my job was to keep Du busy. He loved Obedience training and learned the skills easily. By 18 months of age he had qualified for the Gaines' Regional, which is now known as the Pupperoni Regional. The competition is considered to be the National Obedience Championship competition.

"Eighteen months is a young age to qualify for the two-day regional event, but off we went to New Mexico where Du and I competed in three Novice runs consisting of individual exercises and group stay exercises. After the third set of individual exercises, we were in third place out of 70 dogs, but there was one set of stay exercises remaining.

"As you may have guessed, Du went down on his sit-stay right in front of my eyes. When we came out of the ring, I kneeled down, gave Du a big hug and apologised to him because I knew I had failed him somehow. Of course, I was disappointed, but I had learned that static exercises like stays are more difficult for high-powered dogs like Du. Nowadays my everyday training includes having my dogs stay put in whatever position I leave them.

"During his Obedience career, Du earned an Obedience Trial Championship, two perfect 200 scores, and the affection and admiration of many spectators and friends. He is now nine years old and is in his retirement years, but his face still radiates with his love for life and he has a 'Go get 'em' attitude.

"I am now training my second Bomber son: a four-year-old named Solo. Like his brother, Du, Solo began his Obedience career by qualifying for the Novice division at the Pupperoni Classic. By the end of his third run, Solo had dropped only 1.5 points out of a possible 600. And although the stay exercises are still a bit nerve-racking for me, Solo passed with flying colours and went on to win the Novice division. What a thrill! I am hoping he will become my third Obedience Trial Champion.

"Much of my training time is spent on my eight-year-old Border Collie, Easy, who is my second Obedience Trial Champion. Why train two different breeds? I enjoy both the similarities and the differences. Goldens have a very happy-go-lucky attitude. Both of my Goldens come from

Debby working with Solo.

hunting/Obedience lines and are extremely fast, agile and athletic, and they love to do anything asked of them. They both learn quickly and are not afraid to try anything.

"The fact that Goldens love everyone can be a curse as well as a blessing. Their very sociable nature means extra work must be done on attention and focus, so that they are not distracted by friendly-looking judges, spectators or ring stewards.

"On the other hand, Border Collies seem to be more intense and serious about their work. Perhaps the Border Collie 'eye' that enables them to focus so intensely on stock also enables

them to remain more focused and intense on other tasks.

"All my dogs love to work and we enjoy lots of games and play in our training sessions. The games help relieve stress and keep the fun in training. Obedience training gives us the freedom to take long runs and swims, because I know that the dogs will come immediately when I call them. Everything we do, whether it is running, swimming, herding, Agility, fieldwork or showing, starts with a solid foundation in Obedience. Training is a way of life for us. It is something that adds to our relationship and bonds us as a family."

and then command him to fetch the dumb-bell. You do not necessarily have to give the dog a treat or praise for waiting, as the reward is being allowed to run off and fetch his 'toy'. Praising just prolongs his fun.

- Gradually extend the length of time your Golden is expected to wait.

- If he doesn't wait, do not reward him until he does. If he still refuses to wait, put him on a lead so that he cannot run off.

- Tell him to wait, throw the dumb-bell and release him after a few seconds, then praise him when he comes back with it.

- Repeat until he stops straining on the lead when you throw the dumb-bell. Then you can start practising with the lead off.

Stays

Goldens want to be close to their owners. It is

The Stand-stay is one of the harder exercises to teach.

therefore crucial to build up their confidence so they are happy to perform a Sit-, Down- or Stand-stay for any length of time. In advanced UK Competitive Obedience, a dog is required to Down-stay, with the owner walking out of sight, for an agonisingly long ten minutes. The maximum length is five minutes in the US.

Teaching The Exercise

- Your Golden must be absolutely sure that when you put him in a Stay and walk away, you will always come back. Start off very gradually (see Chapter Two), extending the distance and length of time, a little bit at a time. If, for example, your dog won't stay for 30 seconds, keep practising at 20 seconds, then 25 and so on.

TOP TIP

Stand-stays can be difficult to teach – especially if the dog has to stand for any length of time. The natural reaction is to sit or lie down when waiting for further instruction. Some competitors find it useful to take their Golden pup to ring training classes and to exhibit the pup at shows. Not only does it get the dog used to being in the ring, but it also gets him used to the Stand position, which is useful preparation for when he is required to do a Stand-stay later on.

- Give a reward every time he gets it right, and be really enthusiastic praising him. Before you know it, he will be staying for a minute or more.
- Build on the trust between you, so that eventually you can walk out of sight and your Golden will remain in the Stay until you instruct him otherwise.

Scenting

As with all areas of training a Golden, you should teach scenting by making it an enjoyable game. Hide a toy under a cushion or behind the curtains and encourage the puppy to find it.

Teaching The Exercise

- Show a knotted sock or toy to your dog, shaking it around to arouse his interest, then put it in among a selection of objects which he shows no interest in – mugs, spoons, small pan, etc.
- Ask him to find his toy – you probably won't have to ask twice.
- Once your Golden gets the idea of the game, you can start substituting the items one at a time. Eventually, you will be able to put in other objects, secure in the knowledge that your dog will fetch only the one you have taught him to (i.e. the one with your scent on).
- Make him feel very clever and special when he brings you the correct item.

QUICK STEP

Heelwork to Music, or Canine Freestyle, is still

Goldens have an excellent sense of smell, and tracking comes very easily to them.

a fairly new activity, but is becoming increasingly popular – particularly in the US. Developed from Obedience moves, a dog and handler 'dance' together to a piece of music. Each performance varies, but usually the dog accompanies the owner around the ring in the heel position, turning and moving in time to the music. Dogs also spin, jump, and weave between the owner's legs – the list is endless, dependent only on the handler's imagination.

Not yet recognised by the Kennel Club or the American Kennel Club, the rules of the sport depend on the organisation that puts on the show. Performances in the US can last from a couple of minutes to about six minutes. In the UK, most last between three and four minutes. Competitors can usually perform any music they choose, as long as it falls within the time-frames

Canine Freestyle/Heelwork to Music is becoming popular on both sides of the Atlantic. Photo: Sara Nugent.

given. The ring size may vary but is generally about 40 ft by 80 ft.

The scoring system again depends on the Freestyle organisation or association, but usually includes Technical Execution (degree of difficulty, and dog/handler precision) and Artistic Impression (choreography, costume, synchronisation, etc.).

MFXI (Musical Freestyle Dog Excellent Individual) is the most prestigious title for the sport in the US, and is awarded by Musical Canine Sports International, a Canine Freestyle organisation that was founded in Canada. The first two Freestyle competitions ever held in the US were judged by their rules and guidelines. No title is on offer yet in the UK.

There is a slight difference between the UK and the US. In the UK, the sport is referred to as Heelwork to Music, and the emphasis is more on precision and accuracy. In the US, Canine Freestyle is more flamboyant and creative, a trend that is beginning to be seen in the UK now.

In A Spin

Getting your dog to spin on the spot is fairly easy once you have found out what really motivates your Golden. For these exercises tug-toys will be referred to, but if treats or balls work better for your Golden, use them instead.

- Get your Golden really focused by playing a game of tug.
- Shake the tug-toy in front of him and then move the toy round in a left-hand circle, encouraging your dog to follow it.
- As he is following the toy, say 'Twist', or whatever command you choose to use.
- Every time he completes the exercise, have a good game of tug with him as a reward.
- Repeat the exercise regularly until the dog becomes more proficient, then hide the toy in a pocket and lead the dog with your hand instead, continuing to repeat the word 'Twist'.
- Eventually, he will respond to the word alone and will no longer need guiding.
- Repeat all the above, this time making a right-hand signal. Some people use 'rick' as a command, though you may like to choose your own word.

Under Your Legs

This is quite an impressive move and requires a good degree of co-ordination between dog and

SMILE

When choosing the command words for the different moves, remember that, like a ventriloquist, you must be able to say them in a competition environment while maintaining a smile. Saying your commands discreetly will add to the overall presentation of your performance and may earn you extra points.

owner. As with the spin exercise (above), you must get your dog's attention by motivating him first.

- Have a game of tug. When your Golden is really eager to play, put one leg in front of the other, bend slightly and pass the toy through your legs, encouraging the dog to follow.
- As he is going through, give your command 'Under', and reward him with a game once he has completed the move.
- Once he will follow the toy under your legs quite easily, progress to two steps – passing the toy first under one leg, and then taking a step forward and passing the toy under the next.
- Practise the exercise regularly until you are able to withdraw the toy and guide the dog with a hand. Eventually, the command 'Under' will be all that is required.

Over

Training your dog to leap over your legs is quite a standard move in Canine Freestyle.

- Set up a little jump for your dog in the garden. Perhaps put a broom-handle across two fairly low chairs.

- After a game of tug, encourage your Golden over the jump by standing the other side and tempting him with the toy. If he runs under or around the jump, put him on a lead to gently guide him over (see the Agility jump exercise on page 73).
- When he jumps, say 'Over' and reward him with a game or a treat.
- Keep practising until he will confidently respond to the voice command alone.
- You can then go on to train your Golden to jump simply by holding the broom. Reward him handsomely each time he does so.
- Progress to sticking your leg out in front of you and putting the broom on top of it. Give the Over command and have a game when he does so.
- Once he is leaping your leg and broom reliably, remove the broom.
- You can then practise getting your Golden to leap one leg and then the other as you march.

Once you have mastered these moves, experiment with a few of your own. You can then try choreographing it all to a short piece of music. It's great fun for dog and owner alike – and it's good exercise, too.

ROCK 'N' ROLL OVER

Canine Freestyle is very popular with Golden Retrievers. The most famous example is Rookie, a six-year-old Golden from Houston, Texas, who is owned by Carolyn Scott. Rookie is the first dog that has earned a Freestyle title (MFXI) in the United States. He has made numerous appearances on TV and has become something of a star in the dog world.

"I had been training Rookie in Obedience for a few years when I saw a tape of the very first Freestyle demonstrations done in the US. These demos mainly consisted of heelwork to music. I fell in love with the idea of combining music and dogs together and knew right away that I wanted to give Freestyle a try.

"I decided to refine and lengthen my standard Obedience moves. For example, I taught Rookie to walk backwards in heel position for very long distances. I also taught him non-standard Obedience moves, which I call flash moves. For example, Rookie spins in heel position, weaves through my legs, back away from me across the ring and spins on his own, etc.

"In my opinion, Obedience and Freestyle go hand in hand. An expression I use all the time is: 'Freestyle is Obedience with attitude'. The standard Obedience moves I taught Rookie before we ever started Freestyle strengthened our performances and gave me more choices of movement that I could choreograph into my performances.

Carolyn Scott and Rookie in action.

Photos: Sara Nugent.

"I choose music that matches Rookie's natural movement, along with his personality. Most of our music has been rock 'n' roll music, or country music. When I combine all the moves and choreograph them to music, it becomes a dance.

"Rookie is a wonderful partner. Many of my friends and I think he has rhythm and looks as if he is dancing to the music and is participating in the dance, not just doing Obedience moves. Rookie has a natural talent and flair for Freestyle. He loves learning new things and all the attention, treats, toys and praise, as well as meeting the audiences and performing.

"I always tell my audiences that I choreograph the performances, but Rookie has the final say and adds in his own flair sometimes by doing a few of his favourite moves as we are performing. He is a wonderful showman, very friendly and outgoing, and loves all the attention.

"When people see Rookie perform, they love it and get very excited. Many think Rookie looks like he is really dancing and actually moving to the beat of the music. They are amazed and want to know if he picks his own music or do I! Many spectators tell me they get very emotional when they watch us. It brings a tear to their eye to see the teamwork, and they love how Rookie watches me and how much he enjoys performing. His tail wags the entire time and he can barely contain himself. He is a real showman.

"Rookie is very intelligent and fun-loving and so very dear to me. Eager to please, he loves to dance as much as I do. He is a great ambassador for the sport of Freestyle and for Golden Retrievers."

AGILITY ABILITY

Agility involves running your dog through a course of obstacles within a set time and with no faults. The fastest clear round wins. Goldens love any activity that is shared with their owners, and since Agility usually involves racing around in the fresh air, it appeals to the breed's sense of fun, too.

It is essential to have good basic control (see Chapter Two) before you start working with Agility equipment. If your Golden will run with you, and respond instantly to the Recall, it will make things considerably easier when you first introduce him to a course with many other dogs running around.

Teaching Commands

Body language is vital for directing your Golden through the course. This does not simply involve pointing, but turning your body to each obstacle. Your shoulders should always face the piece that you want your dog to head to.

Because speed is the chief consideration, the handler's priority is to run the shortest distance around the course, while controlling the dog through the obstacles. This may mean directing the dog while you are behind him, in which case he will not be able to see your body language. This is where verbal commands are necessary. Naming the next piece while your dog is still in the middle of an obstacle ensures

Athletic and enthusiastic, the Golden Retriever loves competing in Agility.

no time is wasted. Always remain one step ahead, as vital seconds can be lost by a dog turning the wrong way because the handler didn't direct him in time.

Commands are also needed when 'traps' are laid in the course. Traps are obstacles which are put in the course to test the owner's handling skills. They are often placed immediately after another piece – to make the dog think he should tackle them.

For example, a tunnel may be placed immediately after a succession of jumps, to make the dog think that is the right route, when in fact he is expected to bypass it altogether. Tunnels are often used as traps as most dogs love racing through them. Contact equipment is popular too – especially with Goldens – because lots of treats are used when first teaching it.

There is no standard set of commands for each obstacle. Whatever word you use, make sure it is short or you may lose time on the course.

Opposite are a suggested list of commands which are often used.

To get your Golden familiar with the commands, use the golden rule of opportunity training and 'say as he does'. For example, as he is in the middle of leaping a hurdle, command "Over" or whatever word you have chosen. Your dog will soon realise that the word relates to the action, and he will eventually learn which obstacle to approach according to your verbal command.

EQUIPMENT	COMMAND
Hurdles	"Over"
Long jump	"Jump"
Tyre	"Tyre"
Weave	"Weave"
Dog walk	"Walk"
A-frame	"Ramp"
See-saw	"See-saw"
Tunnel	"Tunnel"

DIRECTION	COMMAND
For the dog to turn to his left	"Back"
For the dog to turn to his right	"Right"
For the dog to be on your left	"Heel"
For the dog to be on your right	"Rick"

WORD OF WARNING

Remember that Goldens should not exert themselves until they are fully grown. The Kennel Club does not allow dogs to compete until they are at least 18 months old. The AKC forbids dogs under one year of age to compete. Until your dog is fully grown, keep long-jumps short and high-jumps low! Also, do not attempt the A-Frame at full height.

The next step is to teach directional commands.

- Teach your Golden to turn left or right by sending him away and getting him to wait.
- Then throw a ball to his left or right. As he turns in the right direction to get the ball, give the relevant command (back or right).
- Practise little and often – on walks and in the garden – as well as at your Agility class.

In the past, Agility was always taught with the dog to the left of the handler, but nowadays dogs run on the left or right, depending on the quickest way around the course.

Teaching the dog to be on your left or right should be approached the same way as with Obedience heelwork (see exercises on page 62-63). A close, tight heel is not required for Agility, but the exercises will get the dog used to coming to your side. Once he is happy on the left side, repeat the exercises with him on your right side, repeating the word 'rick'.

TACKLING THE OBSTACLES

Hurdles

Being one of the easiest obstacles, this is one of the first pieces of equipment that is taught.

- Start off with a very low jump. Get your Golden to Sit-stay in front of it and walk around to the other side.
- Call your dog over to you, using verbal encouragement or motivation (treat or toy). As he jumps, say 'Over' and give the reward when the jump is completed successfully.
- If your Golden keeps running around the jump instead of over it, you can put him on a long, loose lead, stand in front, and encourage him over again. After a couple of successful jumps on the lead, he will realise what he has to do, and can then be tried off the lead.
- The height of the jump is gradually raised until the dog can reliably clear the maximum required level. In the UK, this is 2 ft 6 ins (15 ins for Mini-Agility). In the US, dogs are assigned a class according to their height at the withers. The two categories that most Goldens fall into are: 20-inch jump for dogs 22 ins and under, and a 24-inch jump for dogs over 22 ins.
- When the jump gets quite high, it is common for dogs to run underneath the pole rather than spring over it. Adding a second pole beneath the top one can discourage this.
- Progress to training your dog over a series of jumps.

Long Jump/Broad Jump

The long jump is five feet long and is made up of several sections (from three to five), which make up a gradual incline. In the US, this obstacle is known as the 'broad jump' and is made up of four or five sections and four corner markers. The AKC recommends that the sections are placed in ascending order – from the lowest to the highest board – but it is not an essential requirement.

- Start with just a couple of sections, removing the rest.
- Get your dog to sit and stay in front of the jump.
- Stand the other side of the jump and encourage your dog over.
- As he leaps, say your command word 'Long'.
- Reward him with praise, a treat, or a quick play with his favourite toy every time he completes a jump successfully.
- Gradually add sections of the long jump until he can clear it all.
- Don't forget that as more sections are added, your Golden will need more of a run-up to the jump.
- As with the high jump, if you dog runs around the jump instead of over it, a long lead may prove useful.

Rigid (open) Tunnel

The rigid tunnel is ribbed with hoops so that it remains open all the time.

- Scrunch up the tunnel so that it is at its shortest length.
- Sit the dog in front of the tunnel entrance and walk to the other end. You may need an assistant to hold your dog at the tunnel entrance.
- Call your dog through the tunnel, say 'Tunnel' and reward him when he does so. Gradually extend the tunnel's length.
- When he is happy running through the entire tunnel, put a slight bend in it. Bend the tunnel a fraction at a time until it is in the required position.

Collapsible (closed) Tunnel

Made from cloth, the dog has to push his way through this tunnel, so it can be slightly more tricky to teach. The key is to build up your dog's confidence and to take things slowly. The Golden is such a happy-go-lucky breed, and so trusting, that he is likely to take to it quite easily; if you tell a Golden to do something, most will do it without even thinking there is anything to be afraid of.

❛ Start by teaching the obstacles in easy stages ❜

- Fold the cloth right back on itself so your Golden can see through the tunnel, and encourage him through. Praise and reward when he comes through.
- Fold down a small section and call him through. Reward again.
- Once your dog gets accustomed to the feeling of the cloth on him, and realises he has to push through, fold down another

section and repeat until he will happily race through the tunnel's entire length.

Tyre

As with the jumps, keep the tyre low down near the ground to start off with. You can even begin with it on the ground. As your Golden improves, the height can be raised.

- Sit your Golden right in front of the tyre, and walk round to the other side.
- Hold a treat or toy close to your dog's nose. Slowly pull your hand away from him as he attempts to sniff the treat, and coax him through the tyre.
- As he jumps through, say 'Tyre', or another command you have chosen.
- Give him the treat or the toy as a reward when he goes through the obstacle.
- If he is still reluctant, you can attach a lead, and, standing on the other side, encourage him to come through.

Contact Equipment

The 'contact' equipment is so called because the dog has to touch a marked section at the start and end of each obstacle. This is to ensure that dogs are not injured by leaping off from dangerous heights, and that speed does not forfeit accuracy. A piece of equipment is not considered completed until the marked area is touched.

Dogs are usually trained initially to stop on the marked sections. When they improve and tackle the obstacle at speed, they are then more likely to be pre-programmed to make contact with the area. Because treats are often placed on the contact areas to encourage the dogs to stop, contact equipment soon becomes a fast favourite with most Goldens.

See-Saw

Many dogs can feel very unsteady on this piece of equipment, so progress slowly and stay close to your Golden and keep reassuring him.

- Put your dog on the pivot point and praise him when he does not try to jump off.
- When he is happy being on the pivot point, encourage him to take a step forward, down the see-saw. Praise and reassure him the whole time.

Control is the key when tackling contact equipment.

- Over the course of several training sessions, extend the distance he will walk down the see-saw. Reward him with every step initially to build up his confidence. Do not let him walk it on his own until he feels absolutely secure on this piece of equipment.
- You can then progress to training your Golden to walk up the see-saw, negotiating the pivot point and then down the other side. As he walks it successfully, say your command 'See-saw' so he learns to associate the word with the equipment.

A-frame

This piece consists of a steep climb and descent. It has slats to help the dog keep his grip.

- To teach the A-frame, it is easier if it isn't 'A-shaped', so fold it down to make a horizontal board.
- With your Golden at your side, encourage him to run the length of the equipment. Say your command 'Ramp', and reward him when he comes to the end.
- Gradually raise it a fraction at a time, not forgetting to praise him on each occasion, until the frame has quite a marked incline.
- It is important that your Golden continues to touch the marked contact points. At full height, the frame is very high, and your dog could injure himself if he leaps to the ground too early on.
- As your Golden becomes more confident, and the frame is raised, don't forget that he will need more of a run-up to get to the top.

Dog walk

Although you should teach your dog to walk this piece of equipment, eventually he will race along it, so perhaps it should be renamed the 'dog run'. It is quite simple to teach, as long as you take it slowly and build up speed very gradually to maintain your dog's confidence.

- With your Golden at the start of the equipment and you walking alongside him on the ground, walk him up, across and down the dog walk, while giving your command 'Walk'.
- Reward and praise him on completing the obstacle.
- Keep practising, gauging his progress and increasing the speed accordingly.
- Be very careful to ensure your dog touches the contact areas.

Wait until your dog is completely confident before attempting the A-frame at full height.

WEAVING POLES

The weave can be the most difficult piece on the course, and is usually the last obstacle to be taught. There are two ways of teaching your dog.

Method I

- Start with the poles not upright, but at a 45 degree angle. Alternate the poles, so one is pointing to the left, the next points right and so on. Always position the dog so that the first pole is on the dog's left.
- Holding a treat or toy in your hand, lead your Golden through the poles and say 'weave'. Give the treat or toy as a reward to your Golden on completing the weaves as a reward.
- Gradually move the poles upright. As your dog weaves through the poles confidently at each level, move the poles again until he is rhythmically weaving through fully perpendicular poles.

A toy or a treat can be used to encourage your dog through the weaving poles.

Method II

- Move the first pole to the left and the second pole to the right and so on, until you end up with two parallel rows of poles, about 18 inches (45 cm) apart. Encourage your dog to run through them, say 'weave' and reward him at the end.
- Little by little, put the rows closer to each other, so that eventually they are back in the original one-line weave position and your dog is running through them perfectly.

Table

The dog has to leap up on to a table and stay for a count of five. The judge may ask the dog to sit or go down for the stay.

- Teaching this obstacle combines elements from other areas of training. Reliable Sit-stays and Down-stays are a must (see page 66).
- Getting your Golden to stay on the table, rather than immediately leaping off it, should be dealt with in the same way as you teach a dog to pause on the marked areas of the contact equipment (see page 75).

FLYBALL WIZARDS

Flyball was devised in North America about 15 years ago, though it has only been in the UK for about five. It is very popular at shows, as only a small amount of equipment is involved (as opposed to Agility) and it is easy to immediately understand from a spectator's point of view.

Flyball is a relay race for two teams of four

WINNING GOLD

Kathy Donaldson has trained several Goldens for Agility with considerable success.

"I find competitive obedience can be quite static," she says. "There's more precision, but less excitement. Goldens really enjoy Agility. They are highly trainable and biddable, and very accurate, though they are not always the fastest.

"A Golden's concentration can wane – they have a tendency to switch off sometimes, so you really have to work at keeping them motivated and focused. I do this by always keeping the dog guessing as to when or where a treat will appear – maybe after the first jump, or maybe after a whole series of obstacles.

"Motivating a Golden usually involves food and more food, though my bitch from working lines is motivated by a ball. She has a good chase instinct and loves retrieving, so the ball works better than a food treat as a means of encouraging her through the course.

"You can usually tell Goldens are becoming demotivated and you can react to it – it is a slower process. When they are suddenly distracted by something, though, it is full steam ahead and off they go. There is no predicting it.

"Sometimes a dog will do a victory lap when you haven't even finished the course. They just have a few mad minutes and there is very little you can do except wait for them to rejoin you on their run around the ring, so you can finish the course.

"The temptation of food at shows also causes problems, particularly children's ice-creams by the ring-side and the food stalls. They only have to catch a scent and they are off. One of my Goldens did a demonstration at a show with another handler. She took off for the barbecue and refused to come out from beneath it.

"If a dog becomes easily distracted or demotivated, it may be worth giving them a break from the sport. One of my older Goldens, Cas, had an accident which involved a six-month rest from Agility. Once she recovered, I entered her for a competition. She was really raring to go and beat more than 100 dogs to win. That day was definitely a highlight for me."

Kathy Donaldson finds maintaining concentration can be one of the hardest aspects of training a Golden Retriever in Agility.

Waiting for the off: Every second counts in Flyball. This is Featherquest Blackthorn, known as 'Oscar', who is one of the fastest dogs competing in the UK. He is trained by Claire Prosser, who took him on from a rescue shelter when he was 15 months old.

dogs. Each team has an identical course of four jumps. The dogs must hurdle the jumps, trigger a Flyball box at the end, catch the released ball and hurdle back. As the dog reaches the finishing the line, the next dog can start. The team which completes in the fastest time, wins.

If a fault is committed (a dog starts running before the previous dog reaches the line, a ball is dropped, or a hurdle is knocked), then the dog has to run the course again once the final team member has finished.

The height of the jumps is fixed to the size of the team's smallest dog; most teams have a short-legged dog – such as a Jack Russell – so the jumps will be easier for the rest of the team. The jump is placed four inches below the smallest dog's height at the shoulder. If that dog is 16 inches, for example, the whole team will hurdle 12-inch jumps. The minimum height is 8 inches, the maximum is 16.

The most popular breeds in the sport are: crossbreeds, Collies, Jack Russells, Labradors and, of course, Golden Retrievers. Whatever the breed, competing dogs must be very fit and agile to do well in Flyball competitions. Each dog has to race more than a 100 feet (51 feet there and back), incorporating the jumps and the catch. Amazingly, the team world record is 16.2 seconds, held by Canada. Only two other countries have achieved scores of under 17 seconds: America and the UK.

CLICK AND TREAT

Some dogs are scared by the noise the box makes when a ball is released. Being gundogs, Goldens are not usually intimidated by noises, but if yours doesn't get on with the box, ask your club if you can take it home for a week. Reward your dog every time the box clicks and act relaxed when it makes a noise. Do this for short periods at regular intervals. Within a week, your Golden should be over his phobia – in fact, he will probably look forward to the click as he will associate it with receiving treats.

FLYBALL TRAINING

Break the course down into manageable sections to make it easier to train. Start with the jumps and then the box before introducing other dogs and training the team as a whole.

OVERCOMING HURDLES

- Most training clubs teach the 'restrain recall' for hurdles. For this, you would sit your Golden in front of the jump and another person would hold your dog, while you walked to the other side.
- Use treats, toys and verbal encouragement to persuade your dog to jump over the hurdle to reach you – and the rewards. The other handler should obviously release the dog at this point.
- As your Golden leaps, give your command word, such as 'Over'.
- Praise and pet him when he completes a jump.
- Keep practising until your Golden will respond to the verbal command alone.
- If the dog runs under or around the jump, use the same trouble-shooting measures given for the Agility hurdles (page 73).
- Once your dog is confident jumping a hurdle by voice command, use the same training methods to introduce a series of two, then three, then four hurdles.
- Your Golden should get faster with regular practice, especially if he is fully motivated and raring to go before being allowed to tackle them.

Catching The Ball

- Once your dog has mastered the series of jumps, stand at the end of the row, ready to give him a tennis ball once he has leapt them all. Offer him the ball to hold in his mouth, and give the command 'Hold'. Being natural carriers, Goldens usually have no problems taking and holding balls.
- Turn him, and instruct him back over the jumps to the finishing line, running alongside him if necessary.
- Over the course of several practice sessions, gradually move back, until you are standing behind the Flyball box and giving him the ball from above it. This means your Golden

TEACHING BOXES

There are two types of boxes in the UK. The North American box, which has a pedal making up the whole front face, is used 90 per cent of the time. The dog effectively uses the box as a springboard to turn and continue back down the course, and releases the ball while doing so. The ball comes from the same panel.

The other type used is the Kennel Club box which is used at events such as Crufts. It has an arm at the back of the box, which releases a ball once the dog triggers the pedal at the front. This means there are two phases to the dog collecting the ball – trigger and wait. The North American box has a more immediate response to being triggered.

Oscar in action – the pace is fast and furious.

will have to jump on to the box to reach the ball.

- Over further training sessions, gradually lower your hand until your Golden has to stoop down to get the ball from your hand. Eventually, he should be taking the ball from your hand right by the Flyball-box hole where balls are expelled.

- Once your dog expects the ball to be in that position, you can start using the box. Adjust the equipment so the ball comes out fairly slowly. Speed up as your Golden becomes more proficient.

Team-Work

Only when your dog can race the course with confidence should you start training with the other dogs in the team. Considerable trust needs to be developed among the dogs before they reach competition level, so take things slowly – particularly when working on making the handover more precise.

Eventually you should reach a situation where the two dogs meet on the line – one starting and the other finishing. Both dogs should be at full speed. Flyball dogs do not start running at the line, they usually start about 30-50 feet behind it so they build up speed before starting the course. With another dog running flat-out to return to the line, it can mean two dogs are racing practically head-first at each other at tremendous speeds. This behaviour is very rarely seen in dogs and can be quite intimidating for them if the trust is not developed first. Start with very gentle change-overs, increasing the speed and length of run-up very gradually.

FLYBALL TITLES

There is only one title in the UK. To become an Advanced Flyball Dog, 5,000 points have to be earned. Points are awarded according to the time that the (clear) course is run. For example, under 20 seconds is worth 25 points, and under 22 seconds is worth 5 points.

In North America, there are various titles. A dog can be classed a Flyball Dog when it has just 20 points. It can then go on to become a Flyball Dog Excellent with 100 points and a

Flyball Dog Champion with 500 points. The Silver Milestone is awarded when the dog achieves 10,000 points and the Gold Milestone at 15,000 points. The Onyx award is given at 20,000 points, and is named after the first dog (a Dobermann) to win it.

In North America, points are awarded as follows: 1 point given if the team runs a clear course under 32 seconds, 5 points for under 28 seconds, and 20 points for under 25 seconds.

HOORAY, HENRY!

Pat Hillier has been competing with her Golden Retriever, Henry, for about three years. He has defied all the odds to become a great success in competitive Flyball.

"It was touch and go with Henry when he was just six months old. He had a cancerous growth on his shoulder and we were not sure if he was going to make it. He was given just a 50 per cent chance of surviving the operation. Because of this experience, our philosophy was (and is): if Henry enjoys doing something, let him do it.

"Henry likes being active, so we tried him at Agility. He did very well, and got several placings. He was 'head-hunted' for Flyball after someone spotted him at Agility. They were looking for another dog to complete their team, and as soon as they saw how fast Henry was, they invited him to join. He is such a fast learner, that we were competing after just three training sessions. I couldn't believe our luck – we won the title at the first attempt!

"Henry has had success after success. He was voted by the British Flyball Association the Top (Non-Collie) Flyball Dog, and was the top Golden in the sport. Even though he is getting a little older now – he is seven years – he is currently the highest ranking Golden in the UK.

"Henry earned his Advanced Flyball Dog title when he was five-and-a-half years old. To gain this title, the dog has to be awarded 5,000 points. This is no mean feat, especially if you consider that, in order to win 25 points, the team has to run under 20 seconds; 5 points are awarded under 22 seconds and so on.

"Henry loves retrieving. In the winter, when we don't get out so much, I hide objects around the house for him to find to keep him active. He enjoys Working Trials for the same reason – he just loves fetching things back to me!

"Henry was so quick at getting the ball, he went through a stage of nipping over to the opposition's box to get their ball as well! We had to work really hard to stop this, and, by chance, found that if we put our bucket of spare balls so Henry could see it as he came back over the jumps, he would run even faster to see how many balls he could get out of his bucket. He often manages to get three or four balls in his mouth

Pat Hillier working with Henry

"He is extremely well at the moment, and there has been no recurrence of the cancer, which is the most important thing. He is such a fun dog, he always enjoys life to the full. He regularly gets applauded by the crowd when we compete at shows – everyone can see how happy he is when he comes back with the ball.

"We have so much fun together. For Henry, Flyball is a way of letting his hair down. He doesn't have to think about it in the same way as he does when he is taking part in Working Trials; it is just a great way of him expending all his excess energy.

"Everything Henry does, and every day he spends with us, is a bonus as we didn't expect him to reach his first birthday. And if Flyball is making his life happier, we will carry on doing it."

Safety Measures

Only regulation tennis balls in mint condition are used in Flyball. As soon as a ball is punctured or becomes soft, it is replaced.

Never throw a tennis ball in the air for your Golden to catch. If he tilts his head up to grab it, and opens his mouth, there is a possibility it could go straight down his throat.

According to Flyball organisers, there has been no known case of an accident in the sport involving a tennis ball. Since the ball comes from the side – not from above – it is unlikely to be propelled down the back of the dog's throat. Balls are not released at any great speed, only reaching about two feet if left.

Working Golden Retrievers tend to be slighter in build and darker in colour than those exhibited in the show ring.

THE WORKING GUNDOG

Working Tests are not just for dogs from working lines. Many pet people get bitten by the bug, too. It is a great way of stirring your Golden's natural instincts to work and of keeping him – and you – mentally and physically active. It is a matter of choice whether you progress to Field Trials, where live game is used; so if you do not approve of hunting or shooting, do not let this put you off. It is just as rewarding for the dog to work with canvas dummies.

Goldens from working lines look very different from the show variety, and often get confused for Golden-crosses. They are often much smaller and of a finer build, and are usually darker (to aid camouflage). Their legs are usually longer and they may not have as much coat as the show dog. Faster and more agile, these dogs usually do well in Competitive Obedience and Agility as well as in working tests.

Pet and show dogs are just as able to take part and enjoy themselves, as the same instincts (if a little diluted) are present in all Goldens. Pet dogs may not do as well in competitions, as they are likely to be heavier and therefore slower, but they can still have a lot of fun. In

SHOPPING LIST

If you want to try your hand at Working Tests, you will need:

- A gundog whistle
- A variety of different sized canvas dummies
- A rope slip-lead, which is easy to put on and remove.

terms of character and temperament, there is little difference between the working and show varieties – both have the unmistakable Golden personality.

Getting Started

Formal training for working gundogs does not start until the dogs are at least six months old. Since it depends on the dog's maturity, some start even later. Before this age, your pup will be physically and mentally unprepared for the strenuous activity and absolute concentration that is required

Since basic obedience (reliable Sits, Stays and Recalls) is the fundamental core of all future gundog training, you can start training your pup as soon as you get him home (see Chapter Two). Your Golden also needs to learn how to walk to heel on a loose lead, and then to continue in the same position when off the lead. You do not need to achieve the type of heelwork required in Competitive Obedience – where the dog is virtually glued to your leg. You need your Golden to be close to you, while he is still able to see what is going on around him. As soon as he has completed his course of puppy

vaccinations, enrol at a good pet obedience class to master these skills.

Sock It To Him

Some enthusiasts nurture their dogs' retrieving instincts by throwing soft objects for their young pups to retrieve. It is a good idea to have a bag of items (a knotted sock, a tennis ball, a small plastic bottle covered with a sock), which are *your* toys. The puppy learns very quickly that every so often your toys are brought out and you can both play together, according to your rules. He should not be allowed to play with these toys on any other occasion. He has his own toys, of course, which he can play with as and when he likes.

- Throw the sock just a small distance away and ask your pup to 'bring it to hand' – i.e. to bring it to you. Golden owners know that pups need little if no encouragement to carry such items in their mouths.
- Persuade him to bring it to you by using the same recall methods described in Chapter Two (see page 29).
- You can then progress to six-inch (15 cm) canvas puppy dummies.

All the items the pup is asked to retrieve should be soft. The breed was originally bred to retrieve game – a dog that mouthed a bird rendering it inedible, was no use at all. Wooden dumb-bells and other hard objects should be discouraged for this reason, as it is difficult to correct a hard mouth. On the other hand, a dog that is too soft-mouthed and keeps dropping things will usually learn to grip a little harder.

First Class

When he is ready for formal training and has already mastered basic obedience, contact your Kennel Club or breed society to find your nearest retriever gundog class.

One of the first things your Golden needs to learn is to be trained to the whistle. Special gundog whistles are available that come in different pitches. Your Golden needs to be able to recognise the sound of your whistle so he can respond to the commands that come from it. Blowing the whistle in different ways can tell your Golden that you want him to stop, sit, come and so on.

As with all forms of training, the reward-based method is kinder and more effective than those based on punishment and fear. However, gundog trainers do not usually use food rewards

The working instinct is very strong, as can be seen in this 12-week-old pup who carried out a perfect retrieve without any formal training. Photos: courtesy of the Frisbie kennels.

NOSE TO THE GROUND

A Golden works very differently to the Labrador Retriever. When scenting out the dummy, a Labrador usually works with his nose to the ground. Like the Flat-Coated Retriever, the Golden's exceptional nose means he 'air-scents'. With his head high, he can pick up scents without having to stoop to the ground.

as this encourages the dog to drop the dummy in anticipation of a treat. Dogs are expected to keep hold of the dummy until told to "Give" it (this relates to the dog's gundog background, where letting go of a wounded bird meant the bird usually escaped). Praise is used instead of treats, though Goldens so enjoy working that the retrieve is usually a reward in itself.

Steady Does It

With dummies being thrown, a plethora of new smells and other dogs around, training in a working environment can be incredibly exciting for a novice. Never one to enjoy sitting still, even the most well-behaved Golden might find his self-discipline stretched to the limit. Many will just want to race off and retrieve as soon as they see a dummy thrown. Your ever-eager Golden needs to be taught not to retrieve unless instructed to do so.

Steadiness training involves making your Golden sit and wait – no matter what is going on around him.
- Ask your dog to sit, then throw a dummy.
- Leave it there, and throw another dummy, again making your dog sit and stay.
- Pick up the dummies yourself and throw them again.

- Keep throwing and picking up the dummies, randomly letting your dog fetch one occasionally. Your Golden will soon learn to wait for instructions before retrieving an object.
- If he breaks the stay and fetches the dummy without being told, do not reward him. Start again and withhold praise until he does it right.

Sense Of Direction

In training class, you will also learn how to teach direction to your Golden. Firstly, the dog learns to go away from the handler in a straight line. The command for this is usually 'Go back'. Then he learns to follow hand signals to direct him left or right ('Get on' is often used).

Teaching direction can be a very difficult and lengthy process. Perseverance with the training classes is well worth it: when your dog is fully competent with direction commands, you can progress to sending your dog over long distances – through a field, over a fence, through another field, over a lake, into a forest and back. Since the dog does not know where he is going, trust is crucial. Once in the near vicinity you can command your dog to hunt out and find the dummy.

The working gundog must get used to holding a variety of different textures.

Field Work

If you intend to train your dog to the gun, he needs to become used to holding a variety of different textures. Enthusiasts cover dummies in rabbit skin and bird wings. Your Golden also needs to be accustomed to gun-fire. Training classes usually begin with a starter pistol which is fired at some distance to the dogs, getting closer as they realise there is nothing to fear.

The Golden is not a nervous breed, and is much less likely to be gun-shy than a breed that does not have gundog blood coursing through its veins. Early socialisation where you gradually introduce the pup to increasingly loud noises is invaluable whether you intend to take your dog shooting or not. It means your Golden won't hide under the table for a week if you drop a saucepan on the kitchen floor, and that he will remain calm through thunder or fireworks.

Hunting Competitions

In America, Field Trials reached such a high level that many people, who enjoyed working with their dogs simply as a recreation, were

WORKAHOLICS

Anthea Lawrence first started Working Tests about ten years ago, after a show friend encouraged her to get involved:

"I had always had an interest in Working Tests, but didn't know how to get started. Once I was pointed in the right direction, it was a natural progression from there.

"I joined a local Retriever training class with Roly, my show-bred dog. My first reaction was, 'Everyone is so clever; I'll never be able to do that with my dog!' But gradually you realise that it's not *that* clever; in fact, it's quite achievable – even for a raw beginner.

"The main problem I encountered was having to undo all the problems I had unwittingly created by not starting training early enough. I wish someone had told me not to throw balls and sticks for Roly when he was a puppy. He learned to run off to retrieve a ball as soon as it was thrown, but steadiness (see page 86) is a major aspect of gundog work and I had to undo what he had been taught.

"You have to stick with it, but you start to see some rewards for your hard work quite quickly. At a basic level, you have a much more obedient and responsive dog. The dogs love it, and they associate that enjoyment with going out with you, which strengthens the bond between you. My Goldens seem to know when it is training night. They get so excited, and are almost in the car before I am!

"When working, you are allowing the dogs to do something for you – and working breeds always want to oblige their pack leader. They enjoy seeing other dogs, and if they have met them before, they will lick and greet them. My dogs know their own breed and make a bee-line for other Goldens, ignoring the Labradors!

"There are always disasters, but you are dealing with dogs. If you want something always to work in the same way, you should take up flying model aircraft where you just press the right buttons. Dogs never do what you expect them to.

"Working Tests appeal to all sorts of people.There are a whole range of competitions at different levels you can take part in, but if you are not competitive, you can still take part by being a steward or throwing dummies.

"The enjoyment is also on a social level, because you mix with people who have similar interests. I have made some good friendships through it.

"You go to some lovely places – beautiful estates which host Working Tests – and yet it's not an expensive pursuit. Above everything, I just love watching the dogs. You are allowing your Goldens to do what they do naturally. They love charging around and being in the water. They have a whale of a time."

Anthea Lawrence finds that the relationship with her dog deepens when they work together.

SHOW POTENTIAL

The show exhibitor is looking for a typical specimen of the breed with a sound temperament. Experience plays a big part in spotting show potential – and so does luck!
Photos: Nowell.

Tokeida Man Friday as a baby.

Tokeida Man Friday being taught to stand at eight weeks.

Standing free as a raw six-month-old puppy.

Tokeida Man Friday as a 16-month-old Junior dog – looking good, but still a long way to go before reaching maturity.

unable to devote the time needed to offer serious competition to the more professional trialists. In response to this, the American Kennel Club introduced hunting competitions.

The competitions are not as 'extreme' as Field Trials (which have been likened to a form of doggie Olympics), but more closely resemble real hunting situations. They employ the same skills as Field Trials, but take place over less distance. Competitors are not awarded places, as in Field Trials, but those that finish the course are given 'completions'.

' Show dogs must learn to pose in the ring '

THE SHOW MUST GO ON

Exhibiting your Golden Retriever at shows can be great fun. You will meet other Golden owners – and lots of dogs – and will probably make some good friends along the way. Like all the other canine disciplines, it is a time-consuming activity which takes up many weekends and involves miles of travelling to different shows. Keeping the dog fit, well-muscled and in perfect coat condition also takes considerable time. Competition can be fierce – more so with Goldens because they usually have such a high number of entries.

The major difference with showing is that you cannot improve on what you have got. Although skilled handling and presentation will bring out the best in your dog, he still has to be a good specimen of the breed and conform to the points laid down in the Breed Standard (see Chapter Seven). For this reason, it is important to go to a show kennel and select a puppy that is considered to have show potential. However, you must bear in mind that no breeder can predict a winner, and that as the dog grows, his show potential may never be realised.

If you have an older dog and are thinking of showing, make sure you won't be wasting your time. Of course, in your eyes your Golden is the most divine creature that ever walked on four legs, but he may not quite have what is needed for a show dog. Contact your nearest breed club (through your national Kennel Club) and ask the opinion of an expert.

The budding show dog needs to attend ring training classes so that you both learn what is required. Initially, take your Golden for just 10-15 minutes at a time to get him used to the other dogs. When he is relaxed in this environment, he is more likely to concentrate on his 'proper' training, which entails learning the show pose, the correct way of moving, and being handled by the judge.

Stand And Deliver

Your Golden should stand four square, with his tail level with his back. There are two ways of achieving this in the ring:

- Train the dog to stand freely – this involves the dog standing in front of the handler, who is holding a treat in his hand.
- Stacking the dog – where the handler puts his Golden in show pose and then holds the dog's head and tail in the correct position.

Ch. Tokeida's Outlaw Treasure showing to perfection.

Fun Run

When in the ring, the judge will often ask the whole class to run round in a circle. This will help to settle the dogs and will give the judge a general idea of the dogs in the class. The judge will then assess each dog individually and is likely to ask you to run your Golden up and down in a straight line, or in a triangle, to assess the dog's movement according to the Breed Standard (see Chapter Seven). The Golden Retriever must move at a steady trot alongside his handler, neither pulling in front nor lagging behind. The aim is to show the breed's characteristic long, free stride, and so the handler must interfere with the dog as little as possible. Most exhibitors use a show lead, which is very fine slip-lead. The control it gives is minimal, so it is essential that your Golden is well trained for this exercise.

Handle With Care

Before laying a hand on the dog, the judge will look at your Golden's overall appearance. The dog should be well-balanced, have a good coat and be in good condition. The judge will then assess the dog with reference to the Breed Standard (see Chapter Seven). This will involve a thorough physical examination; so your dog must learn to stand still during this process, and accept being handled by a stranger without any sign of protest.

First Show

For details of forthcoming dog shows, contact your national Kennel Club, or check the dog press. Send off for schedules of those you are interested in. It is probably best to attend the first show without your dog, so that you can get a basic idea of what to expect.

THAT'S SHOW BUSINESS

Brenda and John Taylor did not intend to get involved in showing, but they became "completely addicted" after some fun exemption shows.

"We first went to little exemption shows and just stood and watched. Then we started taking part with Sherrie, our first Golden. We had a lot of fun and won a few competitions.

"We continued taking part when we got our second dog, Mac. He was very beautiful and won a few exemption shows, but, like Sherrie, he was not a good show specimen. But everyone was just so kind. We were invited to people's homes to be shown how to trim the coat properly, and Golden Retriever owners at ring training came over to show us how he should stand and move. You hear a lot of stories about how people are not very nice in the show world, but we found they just wanted to encourage and help us.

"We then bought a puppy, Fergus, with the intention of showing him. His breeder persuaded us to enter a Championship Show. We didn't think such shows were for us, and never would have entered, but we were glad we did – he got second place in his first Championship show and qualified for Crufts!

"There is nothing like being at Crufts. John was all keyed up and shaking with nerves, but to Fergus it was just another show. He was on his best behaviour and got a fifth –

very highly commended. We were over the moon – it was as if we had won the lottery.

"You have to be aware of the Golden personality if you are to show the breed. Some Goldens don't like the standing still part – they are too active. Others take it all in their stride.

"A Golden Retriever can be obstinate, strong-minded and strong-willed. If a Golden does not want to do something, he won't. We have also found that a Golden is prone to lose concentration, so you have to keep the dog focused. Before going in, John has a quick jog around with the dog and gives treats to get their attention.

"Most Goldens love the show scene. They are so sociable and they love the attention, particularly when they are benched and people come up and ask if they can stroke them.

"We enjoy it, too. The buzz of being in the ring is great, and you have such pride in your dog. But even if you don't get anywhere, you always take the best dog home with you."

Left to right: Sherrie (14 years), Oliver (7 months), Fergus (2 years), and Oscar (6 years).

In the UK, the Golden Retriever is placed in the Gundog Group. There are a variety of different types of show, including:

Limited: Only members of the organisation putting the show on can take part. The majority of classes will be 'any variety' classes. For example, a Cocker Spaniel, Pointer and English Setter can all compete against each other in the 'any variety gundog' class. They are often small shows, held in the evening.

Open: Anyone can take part. They will have breed classes as well as 'any variety' classes – see below.

Championship: These shows are bigger, as there is more at stake. For each breed, there are two sets of Challenge Certificates or 'tickets' – one for the best bitch and one for the best dog. At the end of all the breed classes, the winners will go into a final class to compete for the ticket. Any dog or bitch that wins three tickets under three different judges, becomes a Show Champion.

Only Championship shows have CCs on offer, the others do not. To become a Champion (as opposed to a Show Champion), a gundog has to gain a Show Gundog Working Certificate to prove he can do what he was originally bred for.

Young dogs can also win what is called a Junior Warrant. This is achieved by winning 25 points for first prizes at Championship and Open shows. A first prize at a Championship show is worth three points, and a first at an Open show is worth one point. The dog must get at least 12 points from a Championship show, together with a minimum of 12 points from an Open show, or from a Championship show where CCs are not offered for the breed. The points must be earned while the dog is between six and eighteen months of age.

In the US, where the Golden is in the Sporting Dogs category, there are also two types of show: 'licensed' shows (also known as 'point' shows because Championship points can be earned), and informal shows (or 'match' shows), where no points are awarded. There are two types of licensed show:

Specialty: Only dogs of a designated breed or grouping of breeds can compete against each other.

All-breed: There are scheduled classes for all breeds. The breed winners are judged within their Groups, and the Group winners then compete for Best In Show.

To become a Champion in the US, a dog needs to win 15 points under three different judges. The 15 points need to include two 'majors' (three-, four-, or five-point awards), awarded by separate judges.

It is probably worth starting your show career with an Open or Specialty show, because entering a breed class and competing against other Goldens will be very good experience.

As your puppy grows and works his way up through different classes and through different shows, you will find that you improve as a handler, too, picking up tips from the other competitors, and learning how to get the most from your dog.

CHAPTER SIX

A SPECIAL BOND

The Golden Retriever was developed to do a job (see Chapter One). His function was to work with humans when they went out shooting. However, as a breed, Goldens have proved to be so versatile that they have entered many other fields of work, too. Among a diverse range of job titles, the Golden now successfully works as a guide dog for the blind, a dog for the disabled, a hearing dog for the deaf, and a therapy dog.

GUIDE DOGS

The intelligent Golden is loving and affectionate, with a real eagerness to please, and these are ideal qualities for the demanding work of a guide dog.

In the UK, Guide Dogs for the Blind Association (GDBA) has trained more than 7,300 dogs. Five per cent have been pedigree Golden Retrievers, and 44 per cent Labrador-Golden crosses. The GDBA selects Goldens because the breed has "a high level of initiative and concentration, an affable and gentle disposition and an acceptable shedding of coat". The Golden is also said to have an excellent memory when it comes to routes.

The breed is also less likely to scavenge food (one of the downfalls of the Labrador).

The Golden Retriever forms a close bond with his owner, and this can make it difficult for him to transfer his loyalty and affection from his puppy-walker to his trainer and finally to his new owner. Careful handling and training, however, can prevent this from becoming a problem.

The Guide Dogs of America organisation has been running since 1948 and about a third of its dogs are Goldens. The breed has been chosen because "they love to work and are so devoted to their masters".

Opposite page:
Cheryl McMannis working with Ripley.

GUIDE DOGS FOR THE BLIND

Ripley certainly fits the bill. He guides actress Cheryl McMannis, who lives in Hollywood, California. Ripley is Cheryl's second guide dog. Her first, Andy, was also a Golden.

"Ripley is like a clone of Andy," Cheryl says. "He's a platinum blonde with straight hair, and long feathering on the tail. Andy was just the same.

"After Andy died suddenly, I didn't think I could ever go through the business of getting another guide dog. Andy had become like an extension of me, and when he died, a part of me died, too. But I was bamboozled by Guide Dogs

A true working team, Cheryl and Ripley are inseparable.

of America, who asked me to come into the school. I thought it was to receive condolences about Andy, but when I arrived, three dogs bounded in – one of which was a Golden Retriever. It was the last place I wanted to be – surrounded by dogs – but the Golden was really persistent and just dropped down on to my lap.

"She was Marcie, a breeding bitch and she became my 'grieving dog', to help me get over Andy, until my next dog was ready for training.

"When I was in training class with Ripley, I said to the instructor, 'This dog is really like Marcie,' though he didn't look anything like her – not even to the touch. Marcie was red, with a curly coat, whereas Ripley was platinum with a very straight coat, but when they looked up the details on the computer, they found that Marcie was Ripley's mum!"

Ripley is the name of the character in the movie *Aliens*. Although Cheryl calls him her 'little alien', there is nothing alienating about him – they have grown inseparable over the last five years.

"I have come to trust Ripley totally. He has my life in his hands. At first, I found it very awkward, and kept thinking, 'I can't believe I'm trusting a dog!', but I've learned to listen to him. Every time we come to a kerb, I will give a command when I think it's okay for us to go forward, but he is allowed respectfully to disobey me. On one occasion in training, we came to a kerb and I asked him to go forwards, but he wouldn't go. I asked again, and he wouldn't. When a car sped by at 85 miles an hour, I realised why he had refused.

"I live in an area where they are building a subway station. The construction is different every day, but Ripley is so easy and adjustable to change that he safely guides me through all sorts of obstacles and man-holes."

Occasionally, Ripley's halo slips, though – especially when it comes to the breed's Achilles' heel: the Golden gut. When Cheryl was performing in the play *Wait Until Dark*, she would perform alone – Ripley would remain in the dressing room. "It is a very physical play and Ripley doesn't understand that when someone comes at me with a knife they don't really mean it," she explains. At the curtain-call, however, Ripley was allowed on the stage to be reunited with Cheryl. Until this moment, the audience would not have realised that she was blind. On the very last performance, just as Cheryl was receiving a huge bunch of roses, there was uproar from the audience. Ripley had made a bee-line for the food props on a table in the middle of the stage. He had looked, but ignored it, every night, but couldn't resist for the final performance.

"As Goldens grow up, they still continue to have puppy qualities," says Cheryl. "Ripley still plays like a puppy, and he is an ice-cube fanatic. If he hears me go to the freezer, he'll be there. Even if I'm finishing a drink at the end of a meal, he'll hear the ice-cubes clinking. When I throw them to him, he'll catch them and crunch them up.

"Each day, your relationship with your dog gets so entwined. As you both grow older, you become inseparable. You become one – a working team. I see it as having a dance partner. When you first start out, you are both awkward with each other, stepping on each other's toes – literally! Then you start matching the other's pace and strides, and you learn to waltz in synchronicity."

THERAPY DOGS

The work of a therapy dog is not complex, in the sense that they do not have specific tasks to perform, but temperament must be 100 per cent. Therapy dogs visit schools, hospitals, nursing homes, and residential homes for the elderly, and so there is a need for gentleness when working with the sick and frail, as well as being outgoing and friendly to encourage interaction.

Pets As Therapy (PAT) Dogs in the UK and Therapy Dogs International in the US have similar success with the Golden Retriever. Both organisations say the Golden is the most popular pedigree dog they use.

Margaret Bramhall takes her three-year-old Golden, Charlie, on therapy visits.

"My husband and I have always had dogs," she says. "We realised as soon as we got Charlie that he had a superb temperament and loved everyone. We thought he would be ideal to work as a therapy dog.

"Charlie was assessed and passed the temperament tests. Soon after, I saw an advert for a nearby nursing home and made contact. Luckily, the manager of the home was a dog owner, so she was very supportive and encouraging about the scheme. I introduced Charlie to her and we were asked to visit the elderly residents straightaway. We now visit every week.

"The owner was so impressed with Charlie, he put a piece in the local paper about him. This led to me being contacted by an elderly lady, from another nursing home, whose cat had just died. She was bereft, had lost all interest in life and felt she had no reason for living.

"She said to me, 'I know Charlie is a dog, but would you please bring him in to see me?' She looks forward to our weekly visits and says Charlie is as much her dog as he is mine. The lady has told her doctor that Charlie is better than any medicine, and the doctor (a dog owner) agrees.

"Charlie and I have worked in schools to show children how dogs should be handled, and have also visited children with learning difficulties. We visit patients in our community hospital, too, and when we walk in, there is so much interest in Charlie. The carers tell me that the interest continues afterwards too – they talk about him after we have left.

"As well as the residents and patients enjoying the visits, Charlie thrives on it. I would not do it otherwise. He loves all the fuss – and the biscuits!

"Golden Retrievers make excellent therapy dogs because they are so friendly, with very decided characters. They appeal to both young and old because they have such smily, happy faces. They can also look doleful, with their big, gorgeous eyes – especially when they want a treat..."

Margaret Bramhall on a visit with Charlie.

DOGS FOR THE DISABLED

Several different breeds are used as Dogs for the Disabled, but Golden Retrievers and Labradors are the most popular and successful. This is because many of the tasks required of a Dog for the Disabled involve typical gundog work – sniffing out an item that the owner wants and retrieving it. Most importantly, they tend to be soft-mouthed with the items they work with.

Allan Roseberry suffers from post-polio syndrome and is unable to walk. His electric buggy makes him mobile, but is no replacement for a pair of legs – or, rather, two pairs of legs. Four-footed Giles, a Golden Retriever, helps to make life that little bit easier.

"I have a pair of double windows in my study," says Allan. "If I want to draw the curtains, I have to get out from my desk, manoeuvre the buggy to the curtains, struggle with them and then get back to my desk. It can take five minutes and a lot of effort." Giles, however, can do it in just a few seconds, simply by running over and pulling a cord which draws both sets of drapes. He also picks up dropped items that are out of reach, switches on the lights and fetches the post.

Giles is also being trained to pull the electric buggy, using a special harness, in the event of the batteries running out and Allan being left stranded.

Allan has had Giles, his first Dog For the Disabled, for a year now. A dog lover, who has owned Labradors and Goldens for many years, Alan finds that Giles is so much more than simply a great help around the house. "He's a magnificent companion," says Allan. "Life without him would be very lonely."

Margaret Miles feels the same way about her Golden Retriever Dog for the Disabled, Maggie.

Golden Retrievers have a high use of initiative and are able to work independently," says Helen McCain, acting training manager. "They are willing and responsive, and have about nine to ten years of working life. And, because they are bigger than Labs, they can be used for stability work." This is where the dog can help to keep the owner steady and balanced.

"When I got her seven years ago, I had not been able to go out on my own for more than four years," she says. "Maggie definitely gives me my own independence. I can go out shopping now, or meet friends in a restaurant."

Margaret has multiple sclerosis and has good and bad days. She uses an electric wheelchair, and, when she first got Maggie, she had no use in her arms at all.

Maggie helps Margaret in all areas of her life: opening doors, getting the laundry from the washing machine, and fetching items.

"Maggie offers love, dependability, company and someone to talk to – and she doesn't answer back, unlike grandchildren!", says Margaret.

Maggie helping her owner Margaret Miles with the washing.

HEARING DOGS FOR THE DEAF

Training dogs to alert their deaf owners to everyday sounds is a concept that originated in America in the mid-1970s. The success of 'The Hearing Ears' scheme soon meant it was adopted in other countries, and now thousands of deaf people around the world are fortunate enough to have a hearing assistance dog.

A variety of dogs are used as Hearing Dogs for Deaf People – crossbreeds and pedigrees alike. The Golden is used because his placid, amiable temperament makes him a devoted companion to a deaf person and helps to give confidence in social situations. Golden Retrievers have proved to be reliable, steady workers in their task-work.

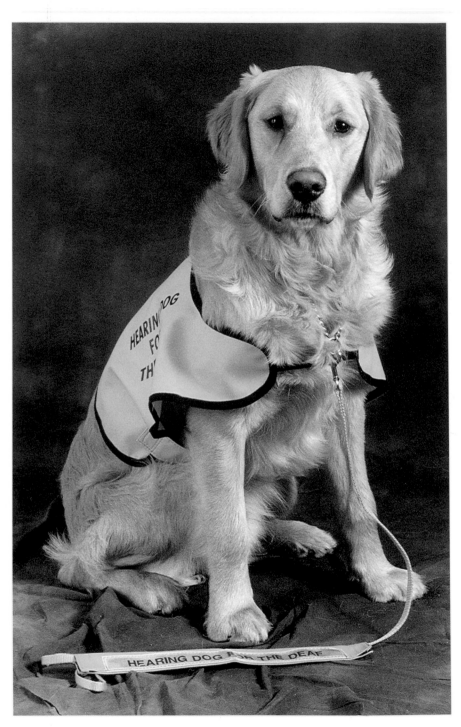

Barnaby, hearing dog for Marjorie Houseman.

BONDING WITH BARNABY

Marjorie Houseman now shares her life with Barnaby, a five-year-old Hearing Dog.

"What a difference Barnaby has made to my life! I use a hearing aid, so I didn't think I could be considered as a recipient for a Hearing Dog. At night, though, when I do not wear my aid, I can't hear anything, so I was eligible.

"Every dog has its own set of sounds. Barnaby's includes: telephone, cooker-timer and the alarm. He has also been taught 'fetch'. If someone wants me at work, they call Barnaby and tell him to 'fetch Marjorie'. He will get my attention by touching me with his right paw. The standard response to this is to ask, 'What is it?'. When he leads me to the colleague, he is rewarded.

"Barnaby works things out in his own mind. A few months after getting him, he pulled me from the path of a van which was reversing which I hadn't seen. I kept trying to pull him back, until I realised what was happening. It is very important to listen to your dog.

"Another time, I was alone in a room at work. Barnaby kept touching me. I said, 'I'll take you out again in a minute,' and told him to wait. But he kept on touching me. When I finally asked 'What is it?', he immediately dropped to the ground, which is his response for a smoke or fire alarm. When I opened the door, I could see everyone was leaving the building as the fire-bell had sounded. It's a sound we don't get to practise very often, but he remembered it. He hasn't been trained to tell me if a pan boils over, either, but he does.

"Barnaby took to my home-life very well. At first, Kira, my Cocker-Beagle cross, had her nose put out of joint and wanted to show she could do everything Barnaby could. Things changed when Barnaby became very ill after falling down the stairs and was in considerable pain. If the phone rang, Barnaby wouldn't be able to get up and tell me. Kira would run up to him to get him to tell me, but she could see he wasn't able to, so would tell me herself. In the middle of his illness, she gave him her favourite red ball, which they formerly had dust-ups over. Kira has since died, but Barnaby still carries it about everywhere.

"Goldens are great diggers – Barnaby and Kira used to ruin the garden together. Food is the other love of the Golden. When I first got Barnaby, he would want my toast every morning. In the end I had to put it in the cupboard until I was ready to eat it as I couldn't stand the sad eyes looking at me. I have slowly taught him not to beg for my food – though everybody else's is fair game!

"One morning, not long after Barnaby's fall, he woke me up. When I asked, 'What is it?', he and Kira both looked at the alarm clock. I got up, fed them and got in the shower. It was only then that I realised how dark it was. I went back to the bedroom to check the time – followed by two well-fed dogs – and realised it was only 4am! 'The clock is not ringing!' I exclaimed. Kira leapt out of her skin and Barnaby just wagged his tail, so I couldn't be angry about their little trick.

"Hearing Dogs for the Deaf always try to match the person and dog very closely. Barnaby and I have similar temperaments. I am a quiet person and Barnaby is gentle and quiet, too. In company, though, he gives me encouragement because he attracts people. Often, they will talk to him before they talk to me.

"I do a lot of fundraising for Hearing Dogs, which entails talking to groups of people. It is so much easier now with Barnaby by my side."

CHAPTER SEVEN

SEEKING PERFECTION

There is an undeniable pleasure in owning a beautiful pedigree dog, and the glamorous Golden Retriever has a huge following of devoted fans. But what goes into producing a litter of puppies that has the true essence of the breed in terms of looks, temperament and physical well-being?

Ideally, every litter should be an improvement on the previous generation, a step closer to the ideal dog as laid out in the Breed Standard.

RAISING THE STANDARDS

A Breed Standard is the written blue-print of the ideal specimen of each breed. It does not mean that every Golden should look the same, but gives general guidelines to ensure that Golden Retrievers remain distinct and retain the typical qualities and characteristics of the breed, while remaining as healthy as possible.

Fashions for different types come and go in every breed, but the Breed Standard is there to ensure that, at its core, the Golden remains unchanged.

In the show ring, judges use the Breed Standard to evaluate each dog. The dog that wins, is the one who, in their view, conforms most closely to the written description. There are minor differences in the Standards drawn up by the American Kennel Club and the English Kennel Club, and where appropriate, these have been highlighted in the following description of the 'ideal' Golden Retriever.

General Appearance

The Golden Retriever is symmetrical and powerful. This is a dog whose function dictates his looks – a working dog, "possessing natural working ability" (KC), "he should be shown in hard working condition" (AKC). Although he should have the body of a hunter, he should also have a kind expression.

Temperament

As well as having a balanced body, the Golden Retriever should have a balanced temperament, too. He should be friendly and confident, and neither aggressive nor shy of other dogs or people.

Head And Face

The skull should be broad. In keeping with a dog who uses his mouth to retrieve game, his muzzle should be wide and his jaws strong. The muzzle should be about the same length as the distance between the stop (the well-defined indentation above the nose and between the eyes) and the occiput (the top point of the head at the back).

Eyes

The dark brown eyes, with dark rims, should be set well apart and convey a friendly expression.

Ears

The ears should be placed approximately level with the eyes, and shouldn't be low, overly pendulous or hound-like.

Teeth

The Golden's teeth should have a complete scissor bite, which means the upper teeth should closely overlap the bottom ones. This is essential if the breed is to maintain its original function as a retriever of quarry.

Nose

The nose should be black or dark brown. A light nose, lacking pigment, is referred to as a Dudley nose. The preference for a darker nose is an aesthetic one: matching the Golden's dark eyes, it makes the face appear more balanced.

Neck

The neck should be muscular and a moderate length.

Forequarters

The legs should be strong and muscular to

The Golden Retriever is essentially a working dog, and this must be reflected in his physique and in his temperament.

The body is balanced, with a level back, and strong, powerful legs.

equip the dog in running or swimming when out on a shoot. The legs should be straight when viewed from the front.

Body

The body should be balanced, with a deep chest and a level topline. The well-sprung ribs should not create a round, barrel shape.

Hindquarters

The hind legs, like the front legs, should also be powerful. The legs should be straight when viewed from behind.

Feet

The feet should be round and cat-like – not long like a hare's foot. Rounder feet are known for

being stronger and will help the dog be more sure-footed. The pads should be thick and hard-wearing.

Tail

The tail should be positioned on, and carried level to, the line of the back. When resting, it should reach the hocks (the dog's ankles), but should not extend beyond them. It should never be curled over the back, or carried between the dog's legs.

Gait

The Golden should have powerful movement, involving long strides and well co-ordinated limbs which move straight forward – turning neither out nor in. All this would have been

The Golden Retriever comes in a range of colours – although the AKC penalises very pale coats.

necessary to help him cover a lot of ground quickly and with the minimum effort when out working.

Coat

The coat may be straight or wavy – it is the quality of the coat that is more important. It should be dense and water-resistant, with a good undercoat and feathering to protect the Golden when running through briar or swimming in a cold lake when out working.

Colour

Both Standards advocate any shade of golden, and both condemn excessively dark coats. The AKC singles out very pale coats as being undesirable, but these are popular in the UK. In both Standards, a few white hairs are permitted on the chest – or on the muzzle if they are the result of ageing.

Size

The KC states that the height at the shoulder

should be 56-61 cm (22-24 in) for dogs; 51-56 cm (20-22 in) for bitches. There is a slight difference with the size prescribed by the AKC: 23-24 in (58.5-61 cm) for dogs; 21.5-22.5 in (54-56 cm) for bitches.

PLANNING A BREEDING PROGRAMME

You can tell a lot about a dog by the way he looks, but what is going on beneath the exterior is just as important. It is essential that all potential breeding stock is subjected to extensive health checks – particularly eye tests and hip and elbow scores (see Chapter Eight: Health Care), and their pedigrees should be investigated for any health problems that may be carried in that line. It is also important that the breeding stock should have the correct temperament, and should be typical of the breed.

The breeder's next task is to find a match of dog and bitch that is most likely to produce typical, healthy Golden Retriever puppies. Again, looks are not the only consideration. Each animal carries their own set of genes inherited from their parents, grandparents, and even their great-grandparents. The skill is to combine the families of both male and female, bringing out the best qualities, improving on any faults, while still ensuring that the progeny is sound in both mind and body.

When breeding pedigree dogs, there are three basic programmes to choose from:
- In-breeding
- Line-breeding
- Out-crossing.

Each programme relates to the degree to which the pedigres of the stud dog and the brood bitch are related. All three options can

Health checks must be carried out on both parents before planning a litter.

The breeder's aim is to produce typical specimens of the breed, that share a similarity in type.

produce sound, typical dogs, provided that the ancestors in each case are typical of the breed in looks and temperament, and are free from hereditary diseases.

The three dogs used to illustrated each type of breeding are Champions or Show Champions, are sound and typical of the breed both in looks and temperament, and have produced winning progeny.

In-breeding

In-breeding is the mating of two very closely related animals, for example two dogs that have the same sire. This type of breeding can be used when you want to accentuate – very quickly – a particular trait associated with that family.

This type of programme is not for the novice, but experienced breeders will know the detailed histories of the dogs involved.

Line-breeding

Like in-breeding, members of the same family are bred together, but they are not so closely related. This is the most common way of breeding and is used to keep the virtues of the line, but introduce new blood at the same time.

Out-crossing

This involves mating totally unrelated dogs. It is often done after a period of line- or in-breeding to introduce new genes and to add new characteristics to your line. Once you have produced the result you were hoping for, you can then fix this type by line-breeding.

Pedigree of Sh. Ch. Elswood The Highlander

Sh. Ch. Elswood The Highlander

The pedigree of this dog illustrates the very close relationships between his ancestors, as his grandmother on his sire's side is a litter sister to the grandfather on his dam's side. His great grandparents are also full sisters.

**Sh. Ch. Elswood The Highlander.
Photo: Lynn Kipps.**

Parents	Grandparents	Great Grandparents	Great Great Grandparents
Sh. Ch. Jobeko Jasper of Nortonwood	Sh. Ch. Nortonwood Silvenus	Sh. Ch. Nortonwood Checkmate	Ch. Davern Figaro
			Sh. Ch. Nortonwood Canellia
		Westley Sabrina of Nortonwood	Ch. Nortonwood Faunus
			Ch. Westley Victoria
	Stirchley Sugarbush of Jobeka	Ch. Nortonwood Faunus	Ch. Camrose Cabus Christopher
			Nortonwood Fantasy of Milo
		Sansue Wanda of Stirchley	Gyrima Moonlord of Rockwin
			Sansue Gillian
Sh. Ch. Westley Clementina	Sh. Ch. Stirchley Saxon	Ch. Nortonwood Faunus	Ch. Camrose Cabus Christopher
			Nortonwood Fantasy of Milo
		Sansue Wanda of Stirchley	Gyrima Moonlord of Rockwin
			Sansue Gillian
	Westley Julianna	Sh. Ch. Lacons Enterprise	Ch. Camrose Cabus Christopher
			Lacons Annaleisa
		Ch. Westley Mabella	Ch. Nortonwood Faunus
			Ch. Westley Victoria

Pedigree of Ch. Westley Gabriella of Siatham

Ch. Westley Gabriella of Siatham

The pedigree of this bitch illustrates the relationship of her ancestors very clearly. The grandfather on the sire's side is her great grandfather on her dam's side.
This is generally believed to be one of the best ways (and one of the safest ways for the novice breeder) of producing quality dogs, provided that the ancestors are line-bred to sound, typical examples of the breed.

Ch. Westley Gabriella Of Siatham.
Photo: Lynn Kipps.

Parents	Grandparents	Great Grandparents	Great Great Grandparents
Sh. Ch. Stirchley Saxon	Ch. Nortonwood Faunus	Ch. Camrose Cabus Christopher	Ch. Camrose Tallyrand of Anbria
			Cabus Boltby Charmer
		Nortonwood Fantasy of Milo	Ch. Sansue Camrose Phoenix
			Sh. Ch. Amber of Milo
	Sansue Wanda of Stirchley	Gyrima Moonlord of Rockwin	Ch. Nortonwood Faunus
			Sh. Ch. Gyrima Pipparetta
		Sansue Gillian	Ch. Sansue Tobias
			Sansue Contasia
Westley Julianna	Sh. Ch. Lacons Enterprise	Ch. Camrose Cabus Christopher	Ch. Camrose Tallyrand of Anbria
			Cobus Boltby Charmer
		Lacons Annaleisa	Lindys Golden Gleam
			Lindys Donnacilla
	Ch. Westley Mabella	Ch. Nortonwood Faunus	Ch. Camrose Cabus Christopher
			Nortonwood Fantasy of Milo
		Ch. Westley Victoria	Ch. Crouchers Leo
			Ch. Westly Jaquetta

Pedigree of Sh. Ch. Ashlyn Piper of Canina

Sh. Ch. Ashlyn Piper of Canina

The pedigree of this dog demonstrates an outcross mating in which there is no replication of dogs on either side of the pedigree.

Sh. Ch. Ashlyn Piper Of Canina.
Photo: Lynn Kipps.

Parents	Grandparents	Great Grandparents	Great Great Grandparents
Sh. Ch. Sinnhein Sebastion	Ch. Sansue Golden Ruler	Ch. Gaineda Consolidator of Sansue	Glenessa Escapade
			Sh. Ch. Rachenco Charnez of Gaineda
		Sh. Ch. Sansue Wrainbow	Gyrima Moonlord of Rockwin
			Sansue Gillian
	Sh. Ch. Sinnhein Minutemaid	Sh. Ch. Nortonwood Checkmate	Ch. Davern Figaro
			Sh. Ch. Nortonwood Canella
		Westley Matthia of Sinnhein	Ch. Nortonwood Faunus
			Ch. Westley Victoria
Ashlyn Emerald	Darris Startime of Canina	Ch. Gatchells Sky at Night	Ch. Camrose Fabius Tarquin
			Gatchells Superkay
		Darris Double Daisy	Thenford Gannymede of Sandusky
			Goldsheen Harmony of Darris
	Ashlyn Holly	Sh. Ch. Pitcote Arcadian of Garthfield	Sh. Ch. Teecon Knighterrant
			Singapore Ch. Lacons Edelweiss
		Ashlyn Summer Heidi	Ch. Camrose Fabius Tarquin
			Willaray Christobel of Ashlyn

PUPPY TO CHAMPION

After all the hard work of researching pedigrees, conducting health checks, and supervising the mating and whelping, the litter is born. For the first few weeks there is little to choose between the individuals – they are all fluffy and cuddly, stumbling around on wobbly legs. But the experienced breeder will soon start making assessments – working out which puppy is most likely to mature into the 'ideal' specimen.

The best laid plans can founder, and sometimes the most beautifully bred litter will produce nothing special in terms of show quality and future breeding stock. Equally, the puppy who looked full of promise at eight weeks may not fulfil his potential, and there is always the 'ugly duckling' phase guaranteed to give the breeder sleepless nights... It is all part of the fascinating business of breeding pedigree dogs.

The following photos have been selected to show the stages of development of a number of individuals who made the grade from puppy to Champion.

Sh. Ch. Tamarley Heaven's Hero

Six weeks old.

Eleven months old. **Photo: David Dalton.**

Nine weeks old.

A Show Champion at twenty months old.
Photo: David Dalton.

Sh. Ch. Darthill Lavender And Lace

Darthill Lavender And Lace aged seven weeks.

Eight months old.

Two-and-a-half years old – and a Show Champion.

CHAPTER EIGHT

HEALTH CARE

BY LARRY ROBERTS (PhD, BVMS, MRCVS)

olden Retrievers are active, energetic dogs, who should live a long, healthy life of between 12 and 14 years. However, some hereditary conditions are creeping into the breed, (hip, elbow, eye and heart problems, see below). To minimise the chances of heartbreak later, you should investigate the parental health of any pup you are considering purchasing. If you have any concerns about your dog's health, you must consult a vet immediately.

PREVENTATIVE CARE

As well as ensuring your Golden receives the correct diet and exercise, routine care, involving vaccination and parasite control, is also important in maintaining your dog's health.

Vaccination

The aim of vaccination is to provide active immunity (produced by the puppy initially and maintained at a protective level throughout his life) as soon as possible. This is complicated by the presence of maternally derived immunity (provided by antibodies acquired in milk from the bitch) which can interfere with vaccination and prevent the development of protective active immunity.

The primary course of vaccination will be between eight and twelve weeks of age. The timing of vaccination and the vaccine used will vary depending on the local situation, such as disease prevalence and other risk factors. The situation is best discussed with your veterinary surgeon.

Following the primary vaccination course, most dogs are revaccinated annually. Some components need to be given annually, e.g. intra-nasal Bordetella bronchiseptica vaccines and dead bacterial vaccines such as Leptospira vaccines. Other components of routine vaccines, such as canine distemper virus, may provide protection for a number of years. Good scientific data is not available for how long immunity will last

Immunity is initially derived from the bitch.

following vaccination.

In recent years, some people have been reluctant to have their pets vaccinated every year, following publicity about the possible adverse reactions that can result in a small number of cases. There is no convincing study which shows a greater incidence of the problems ascribed to vaccine reactions than in the general canine population. Currently, the majority of vets employ a policy of annual vaccination.

There are a number of important specific infectious diseases in dogs for which modern vaccines are available. These include the following:

Canine Distemper is a virus which can result in a wide variety of signs. High temperature, diarrhoea (less commonly, vomiting), coughing, nasal and ocular discharge are all seen. Hard pad is seen in some cases later in the disease, and a high proportion of infected dogs go on to show nervous signs – fits, chorea (regular rhythmic twitching of a muscle group) and paralysis.

Canine Parvovirus (CPV) is a relatively new disease, which emerged in the late 1970s in Europe and spread worldwide. Two forms of infection with CPV are recognised: CPV myocarditis, which results in heart failure and is now very rare, and CPV enteritis, whose symptoms include vomiting followed by diarrhoea of varying severity often accompanied with blood loss. The course of the disease is short and, without intensive fluid therapy, rapid death can occur.

Infectious Canine Hepatitis. Mild cases result in the dog being off-colour, with reduction in appetite and raised temperature. Recovery is usually uneventful. In severe cases, onset of illness is sudden, with the patient being extremely dull with a very high temperature. There is enlargement of the lymph nodes and the tonsils are swollen and reddened. The liver is swollen and the dog develops a bleeding tendency. Dogs recovering from this infection can develop corneal oedema ('blue eye').

Kennel Cough is a disease syndrome which can be caused by several agents (bacterial or viral) acting either singly or in combination. Vaccines are available for the prevention of the commonest of infections. The main, and often only, sign of Kennel Cough is a cough, which is typically dry and hacking. Excitement will often exacerbate the signs. Sneezing – with nasal discharge – or productive coughing can occasionally occur. Coughing may be short-lived (three to four days), but may last two weeks and rarely over three weeks. Typically, the

Kennel cough spreads quickly in a resident population of dogs.

dog's temperature will be normal and the dog remains bright. More severe signs may indicate the development of pneumonia. Although most cases will recover uneventfully in two to three weeks, antibacterial drugs are indicated to prevent pneumonia from developing and spread of infection to other susceptible dogs.

Leptospirosis. A variety of types of Leptospira can infect dogs, but only two of the commoner strains are included in vaccines: Leptospira canicola and Leptospira icterohaemorrhagiae. Infection with other Leptospira strains are being increasingly recognised. Many of these are of wildlife origin, e.g. from mice and voles, and an important risk factor is access to water. Dogs exercised in the country with access to water would be at risk, and Golden Retrievers often fall into this category.

Infection may present as liver or renal failure, but less specific symptoms include general malaise and raised temperature.

Lyme Disease is transmitted through tick bites. The species of tick involved varies between Europe and the USA. Common signs following infection include lameness, high temperature, loss of appetite, lethargy and swollen lymph nodes.

Vaccines are available in some countries to prevent this infection. If you live in an area which has a high tick population or are visiting such an area, then vaccination may be appropriate in advance of exposure.

Rabies is present in all continents except Australasia and Antarctica, although several countries, because of geographical barriers, are free of infection, e.g. the United Kingdom. The virus does not survive long outside the body and its maintenance in countries is by wildlife or stray dogs. Transmission is mainly by biting, and signs relate to infection of the central nervous system. Vaccination is not carried out routinely in the UK but is available under a pet-passport scheme being introduced. This is to allow dogs to travel to other European countries and not be quarantined on their return.

PARASITES

There are several endoparasites (found internally) and ectoparasites (found on the surface) which can be a problem in dogs. Some of these can also cause zoonotic infections – infections in man transmitted from animals.

ENDOPARASITES

Toxocara canis: These are large, round, white worms, commonly known as roundworms, and adults can be 7.5-15 cm (3-6 in) long. All puppies should be assumed to have a Toxocara burden due to the complex life-cycle of this parasite. Roundworm larvae remain dormant in the tissues of adult bitches following ingestion, and during pregnancy they become activated and cross the placenta into the puppy's liver (before birth). Following birth, the larvae complete their migration via the lungs and trachea, and are swallowed and develop into adults in the small intestine.

In late pregnancy and early lactation in the bitch, reactivated larvae also migrate to the mammary tissue and are passed to the puppies in milk. The larvae ingested in milk develop directly into adults in the intestine and do not undergo tissue migration.

It should be assumed that all puppies carry a burden of roundworm.
Photo: Amanda Bulbeck.

Puppies should be wormed regularly, e.g. every two weeks up to eight weeks old and then every four weeks up to six months old. Dosing recommendations for adults vary. Some recommend a minimum of twice a year, others advocate four times a year.

It is more unusual for adults to pass Toxocara eggs in faeces, but it is advisable to worm regularly to reduce risks of environmental contamination. Although this is a very uncommon zoonosis, it can have serious consequences. Suitable worming treatments for this and other worms are available from your veterinary clinic.

Toxocara leonina

This is another roundworm of similar appearance to Toxocara canis, but does not have the same complex life-cycle.

Tapeworms

Tapeworms have indirect life-cycles, so spread is not directly dog to dog, but involves one or two intermediate hosts, which can be either invertebrate or vertebrate.

Dipylidium caninum: The flea is the intermediate host for this tapeworm. Flea larvae swallow eggs shed by the dog which then mature as the flea develops. When the dog consumes an infected flea, the larvae are released and mature into egg-laying adults completing the life-cycle. This worm can measure up to

50 cm (20 in) in length, but it is individual segments which are passed in faeces. These segments resemble rice grains and can be seen on the dog's coat, around the anus, or in the bedding. In the event of infection, flea control should also be implemented.

Echinococcus granulosus/multilocularis: Intermediate hosts for this parasite include sheep, horses, rodents and humans (in which infection can be serious). Infection in sheep in hill areas can be a problem, and it is important not to allow your dog to scavenge from dead sheep carcases.

' Seek advice on correct procedures for worming '

Taenia species: A variety of species are described with different intermediate hosts, e.g. cattle, sheep, pigs and rabbits.

Echinococcus and Taenia infections are only possible if raw meat is fed or your dog is allowed to scavenge, e.g. dead sheep or rabbit carcases. Safe and effective wormers are available from your veterinary clinic.

Hookworms

Ancylostoma and Uncinaria are more likely to be a problem in kennel dogs who have a grass run. Infection is by larval penetration of the skin and can be associated with a dermatitis.

Whipworms

Trichuris is again more common in dogs in runs,

as Trichuris eggs survive for a considerable time in the environment.

Filaroides Osleri

Adult female worms are embedded in nodules in the trachea, causing inflammation. This causes inflammation of the respiratory tract and coughing. The condition is most often seen in puppies and young dogs.

Heartworm

This is transmitted by mosquitoes. Adult female worms can be up to 27 cm (10.5 in) in length. Adult worms are found in the right-hand side of the heart and the females produce microfilariae (i.e. microscopic larvae), which are ingested by mosquitoes when feeding. The microfilariae develop in the mosquitoes and migrate to the salivary glands and, when the mosquito feeds, are passed into a new host. Clinical signs associated with heartworm are those of right-sided heart failure. Control is by the administration of an effective drug during the period of mosquito activity.

ECTOPARASITES

Fleas

Fleas are probably the most ubiquitous ectoparasite of dogs. The commonest flea found on dogs is the 'cat flea', which is capable of maintaining its life-cycle on a number of hosts. Dog fleas are the next most common. Hedgehog fleas are found only occasionally, and human fleas are very rare indeed.

Flea control must include both dog and home environment.

Flea control has to cover both the adult fleas on the dog and the immature stages in the home. Fleas feed on the dog but the eggs fall off the dog, and, after hatching into maggot-like larvae, complete their development in the environment. Development time is dependent on environmental conditions and is faster in warmer conditions, but fleas can survive in suitable environments for up to 12 months without feeding.

A variety of effective products are available to control flea infestation, including insecticides, products which inhibit the reproductive cycle of the flea, and others which act specifically on the insect nervous system. Control in the home should include vacuuming to remove immature stages and treatment with appropriate products.

Lice

Lice are more host-specific and require direct contact for transmission, although shared grooming equipment or bedding could result in transmission. The whole life-cycle occurs on the host and the female lays eggs which are attached to the hair. Infestation is associated with violent itching, hair loss and self-trauma. Insecticidal washes and shampoos are available for treatment. Grooming equipment and bedding should also be treated with an insecticide.

Harvest Mites (Chiggers)

The larvae of Trombiculid mites are parasites, and infestations with these small orange-red mites mostly occurs in late summer and autumn and particularly in animals exercised in fields and woodlands. Affected areas are most commonly the paws, lower limbs and the head. Appropriate insecticidal sprays or washes can be used.

Ticks

Infestation with ticks can be a problem in dogs exercised in areas with heavy tick populations. Ticks can cause local reactions but can also be responsible for transmission of a number of infectious conditions, e.g. Lymes disease. Effective products for their treatment and control are available, some of which have a period of activity of four weeks or longer. In endemic areas, or when repeat exposure is likely, regular treatments are advisable.

Golden Retrievers living in the country are more likely to pick up ticks.

A-Z OF HEALTH PROBLEMS

General health will be considered on a systematic basis, but it must be remembered that any signs in your dog can be due to one of several diseases. So, for example, a dog with increased drinking may have kidney disease, but the increased thirst could also be due to a disease of the endocrine system, such as diabetes mellitus.

Allergic Skin Disease (Atopy)

The most common allergic reaction is to parasites, in particular the flea. Atopic skin disease is the commonest non-parasitic form. Golden Retrievers are one of the breeds in which atopy is most often seen. Atopy is an inherited predisposition to develop allergic antibodies to environmental allergens. Exposure was traditionally considered to be via the respiratory tract, but increasingly the view is that allergen exposure is by direct skin contact with the allergen. Most often, clinical signs develop between one and three years of age, although it is occasionally seen between six and twelve months, and, only rarely, after six years of age. Intense itching is the main feature of this condition and self-trauma and secondary bacterial and/or yeast infections are common.

Allergens are the substances to which the allergic reaction develops and include grass or tree pollens and dust-mites. As exposure to some of these (e.g. pollens) is not continuous, the

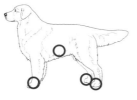

condition may present as seasonal, but in the case of, for example, house dust mites, there may be no seasonal pattern.

Aortic Stenosis

This is a congenital cardiac disease seen in a number of breeds, including the Golden Retriever. It is usually the

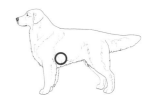

result of a fibrous band which develops below the aortic valve and can affect outflow from the left side of the heart. The severity is variable and mild cases will show no signs and may have a normal quality and duration of life. Severely affected dogs are associated with a shorter life-expectancy and a risk of sudden death.

It has been suggested that selection of dogs for breeding with no detectable abnormalities of aortic stenosis would allow the problem to be controlled. Initial screening is done by listening to the heart with a stethoscope, and this can be followed up with a specialised examination using echocardiography to confirm and identify the severity of the aortic stenosis.

In mild cases, treatment is not necessary. In severe cases, involving heart failure, your vet will recommend specific cardiac medication.

Digestive Tract Diseases

Vomiting is not uncommon in dogs, often as a result of dietary indiscretions from scavenging decomposed

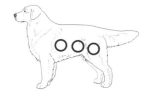

or unsuitable materials. If the vomiting is short-lived and the dog is otherwise bright, no action may be needed. If vomiting persists or the dog is depressed, then veterinary advice should be called on. Similarly, if diarrhoea develops but the dog is still bright and alert, then dietary manipulation may be all that is necessary, i.e. an initial period of restriction followed by a bland diet, chicken, fish, rice, and then gradual reintroduction of the usual diet. If the diarrhoea persists or is recurrent, then veterinary attention will be needed. Further investigations to establish the exact cause may be needed. This could include examination of blood and faeces samples, radiography or ultra-sound scanning. In some cases, tissue samples for examination may be needed and are collected at the time of exploratory surgery of the abdomen.

Elbow Dysplasia (ED)

ED refers to the abnormal development of the elbow joint with problems in the growth of the cartilage and the subsequent development of arthritic changes. Although there is a genetic influence on the development of ED, other factors, such as growth rate, diet and exercise, also have a significant influence.

Dogs with ED often become lame between six and twelve months of age and, initially, the lameness may be intermittent and difficult to localise. However, a persistent front leg lameness should be investigated to ascertain if it is ED. Treatment

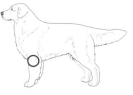

may involve surgery or may be more conservative, with weight restriction and control of exercise. Drugs may be necessary to relieve pain and control inflammation and aid the repair process.

Schemes to grade elbows radiographically are being introduced under the guidance of the International Elbow Working Group. To date, the uptake is much smaller than for the HD schemes, but it may be that the breeder of your puppy will have details of the elbow status of the parents in addition to information on hips.

Endocrine Disease

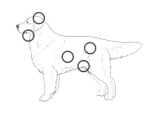

In recent years, our understanding of endocrine disease in the dog has advanced considerably. The commoner conditions seen are hypothyroidism, Cushing's disease and diabetes mellitus, although there are a number of other endocrine diseases also described. Advances in diagnostic tests and in subsequent management have also been made.

Epilepsy

Epilepsy is a syndrome of recurrent fits, which can be primary (caused by an inherited functional problem in the brain) or idiopathic (resulting from injury to the brain that has left residual damage). Idiopathic epilepsy, which is seen in the Golden

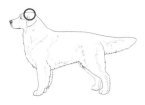

Retriever, is usually initially seen between six months and three years of age. In some dogs, however, seizures are not seen until five years of age.

Eye Conditions

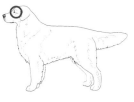

There are a number of inherited eye conditions in Golden Retrievers. Some of these are serious and can result ultimately in blindness, e.g. PRA (see below), but others are not usually associated with a significant effect on vision. In each country there are official schemes run by the national Kennel Club and veterinary associations to promote control of inherited eye conditions through regular eye examinations in breeding animals and removal of affected animals from the breeding programme. In practical terms, this means that when purchasing a puppy you need to check that both parents have current eye certificates, i.e. they have been examined within the previous 12 months and found to be free of those eye conditions considered to be hereditary in the Golden Retriever.

Hereditary Cataract (HC)

Cataract is the term used to describe an opacity of the lens or its capsule. In Golden Retrievers, HC is used to describe a specific type referred to as posterior polar subcapsular cataract, i.e. it is sited at the posterior

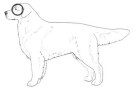

pole of the lens in a subcapsular position. It is usually small with no disturbance in vision.

As well as being an inherited condition, cataracts can also occur for a variety of other reasons, such as injury to the eye, general disease (e.g. diabetes mellitus), or secondary to other eye changes.

In most cases, the dog is not affected at all, so no treatment is necessary.

Congenital Cataract

Present at birth and noticed soon after the puppy's eyelids open, this condition also occurs in the Golden Retriever. When viewing a pup, you would immediately be able to see that it had this condition.

Generalised Progressive Retinal Atrophy (PRA)

Night blindness is sometimes used to describe this hereditary condition. There are degenerative changes in the retina, the light-sensitive part of the eye. Although starting as a loss of night vision, the condition progresses to produce poor vision under all lighting conditions, and pupillary response to light is poor. The pupils are dilated and there is often increased reflectivity from the back of the eye. The condition progresses to total blindness. There is no treatment for the condition.

Retinal Pigment Epithelial Dystrophy (RPED)

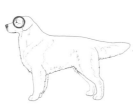

This condition is also referred to as *Central Progressive Retinal Atrophy.* In this condition, there is degeneration of the light-sensitive photoreceptor areas of the retina due to the accumulation of waste products. Initially, affected dogs show reduced vision in daylight, vision in dim light only being affected in the later stages of the disease. Pupillary light response often remains reasonable and complete blindness is unusual.

The primary genetic problem is a defect in the way in which the dog handles vitamin E, and changes to the retina are secondary to this. If identified, this condition can be treated with vitamin E supplementation, which will prevent further progression.

Multifocal Retinal Dysplasia (MRD)

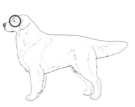

Retinal dysplasia results from the disorderly proliferation and atypical differentiation of the retina during embryonic development. In the Golden Retriever the type seen is multifocal retinal dysplasia. Linear folding of the sensory retina occurs in the vicinity of the optic disc. In the majority of cases, these changes are not associated with significant visual impairment, unless larger areas of retinal degeneration occur or retinal detachment occurs. The latter is rare in the Golden Retriever.

Glaucoma

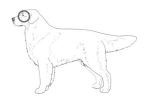

Glaucoma is a condition with increased intra-ocular pressure and it can be primary (i.e. with no other ocular disease preceding its development) or secondary to other ocular disease. A primary glaucoma is recognised in the Golden Retriever and is currently under investigation. Your vet may prescribe drugs to reduce the intra-ocular pressure.

Geriatric Canine Vestibular Disease

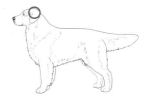

A condition seen in older Golden Retrievers with the sudden onset of head tilt, inco-ordination and falling. It can vary in its severity, with difficulty in standing being a feature of severe GCVD. It is occasionally associated with transient vomiting, nausea and anorexia. There is involuntary rhythmic movement of the eyes which resolves within a few days. The ataxia gradually reduces over one or two weeks, as does the head tilt. Recovery is usually satisfactory. Veterinary attention should be sought to exclude other causes of these signs.

Hip Dysplasia (HD)

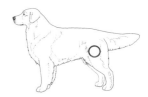

HD is a condition in which there is abnormal development of the hip joints, which ultimately leads to osteoarthritic changes. There is a genetic influence to this condition, but environmental factors, such as exercise and nutrition, are also extremely important. In an attempt to improve hip status in dogs in the UK, the Kennel Club, in association with the British Veterinary Association, has developed a hip-scoring scheme so that stock with better than average hips for the breed can be selected for breeding. This is based on examination of radiographs of the hip joints by a panel of experts. In the USA, there are a number of similar schemes. One is run by the Orthopaedic Foundation for Animals (OFA), another is the University of Pennsylvania Hip Improvement Programme, and a scheme is also offered by the Institute for Genetic Disease Control in Animals.

All breeding stock should have had hips examined radiographically and assessed. In practical terms, this means that before you purchase a puppy you should discuss with the breeder the hip status of the parents and related dogs. You should find out the average breed hip-score (or grade) from your national kennel club, and ideally both parents should have scores below the breed average.

In the unfortunate event of hip dysplasia being diagnosed, treatment options should be discussed with your vet. Conservative treatment includes the control of bodyweight and exercise modification (regular and mild exercise); medicinal treatment covers pain elevation, and drugs that can reduce or reverse changes on the cartilage of the joint; and a surgical option is also available.

Hypothyroidism

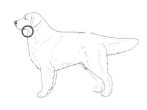

This is an endocrine disorder with a reportedly higher incidence in some breeds, including the Golden Retriever, than others. A deficiency in thyroid hormones causes a decrease in the basal metabolic rate, thereby affecting all body systems. Onset can be insidious and vague, but the commonest signs are lethargy, dullness, unwillingness to exercise, weight gain, dry and scaly skin, hair loss, and secondary skin infections. Many of these signs could also be due to other causes and laboratory investigation and confirmation is essential. It is also important to note that most obese dogs are not hypothyroid.

Pyometra/Cystic Endometrial Hyperplasia

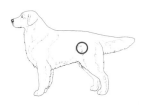

Common in older entire bitches, this has an underlying hormonal basis. It can present as open- or closed-pyometra. With open-pyometra, there is a purulent vulvar discharge which is often tinged with blood. In closed-pyometra, the uterus is filled with fluid and there is no vulvar discharge. Presenting signs are: increased drinking and urination, vomiting and anorexia. It occurs in the eight-week period after oestrus (i.e. the period following a season).

Skin Diseases

There are many different causes of skin disease, including bacterial and yeast infections, parasites (fleas, lice, mange mites), allergic diseases, and underlying endocrine disease, an example of which is hypothyroidism.

It is important to reach a specific diagnosis so that the correct treatment and preventative measures can be implemented. If initial treatment by your veterinary surgeon is not successful, or if there are recurrent problems, investigations into underlying causes will probably be carried out.

Tumours

Early discovery is essential, as is recognising the type of tumour involved so that the most appropriate treatment can be undertaken. When lumps or bumps are located while grooming or stroking your dog, it is advisable to seek veterinary advice.

Urinary Tract Diseases

As dogs age, kidney disease can be a problem,

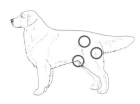

but following early recognition a suitable dietary regime and appropriate medication can be introduced to slow down progression in many cases. Lower urinary tract disease can also be a problem.

In bitches, cystitis is not uncommon and can present as frequent urination, and often blood is present in the urine. In mainly older male dogs, prostatic disease can be a problem and can present as difficulty in urination or pain at urination. Increased urination, as well as being seen in diseases of the urinary tract, may also be due to other conditions, e.g. diabetes mellitus. Veterinary examination will be necessary to determine the exact cause of the problem and to institute appropriate treatment and, if necessary, preventative measures. For example, once bladder stones are surgically removed or dissolved by dietary means, then recurrence could be prevented by feeding a special diet.